COME ALIVE

COME Alive

FIND YOUR PASSION,
CHANGE YOUR LIFE,
CHANGE THE WORLD!

JODI HADSELL

NEW YORK

LONDON • NASHVILLE • MELBOURNE • VANCOUVER

Come Alive

Find Your Passion, Change Your Life, Change the World

Published in New York, New York, by Morgan James Publishing in partnership with Difference Press. Morgan James is a trademark of Morgan James, LLC
www.MorganJamesPublishing.com

ISBN 9781642797664 paperback
ISBN 9781642797671 eBook
ISBN 9781642797688 audiobook
Library of Congress Control Number: 2019913213

Cover Design Concept by:
Difference Press

Cover Design by:
Rachel Lopez
www.r2cdesign.com

Editor:
Bethany Davis

Book Coaching:
The Author Incubator

Morgan James is a proud partner of Habitat for Humanity Peninsula and Greater Williamsburg. Partners in building since 2006.

Get involved today! Visit
MorganJamesPublishing.com/giving-back

*For Chris, who always told me
that my health would not improve
unless I was living a life of passion.*

Table of Contents

Chapter 1:   The Introduction 1

Chapter 2:   My Journey to Passion 5

Chapter 3:   The Come Alive Process and Tools 15

Chapter 4:   Step One: Assess Yourself 23

Chapter 5:   Step Two: Explore Your Archetypes 35

Chapter 6:   Step Three: Tackle Your Challenges 75

Chapter 7:   Step Four: Restore Your Brilliance 93

Chapter 8:   Step Five: Hone Your Desires 103

Chapter 9:   Step Six: Manifest Your True Passion 111

Chapter 10:   You Made It This Far!. 119

Chapter 11:   Your Journey Is Unique 123

Further Reading 127

Acknowledgments 129

Thank You 133

About the Author 135

CHAPTER 1

The Introduction

> *"The two most important days in your life are*
> *the day you were born and the day you find out why."*
> —Anonymous

YOU ARE NOT ALONE

Are you tired of living the dreams that someone else had for you? Are you tired of taking care of others before yourself? Are you sick of putting yourself and your desires on the back burner? Are you stuck in a career or job you hate? Do you feel undervalued, empty? Are you tired of being afraid, of hiding out and not knowing why you can't just seem to figure things out? Are you wanting this to not be your life anymore? Do you feel like it may be too late to change paths, find your true passion and start living it? Time is definitely up on this!

How do you respond when people ask you, "What's your true passion"? Are you like a deer in the headlights? Do you shrink because you don't *really* know the answer, and you're ashamed that you don't know? Do you *sort of* know but you have no idea what to do with it? Maybe you know *for sure* what it is, but you are stuck in a well-paid yet soul-crushing corporate job and you're too afraid to quit and go for what you want. Do any of those describe you? Because they all described me, at different stages of my own journey.

If any of those describe you, you are not alone. Most people do not know what their passion is, or they are not living it. I know because I ask just about everyone I meet that question! When you look at strangers walking down the street, you can usually tell if they know what their passion is. Those who know their passion and are actually living it walk taller, have a spring in their step, look you in the eyes, smile at you, and laugh, a lot. You can just tell they have a fire burning inside of them—that they are fully alive.

Do you know how many people in the corporate world *hate* their jobs? Do you know how much money that costs our country or the world? When people are working in jobs that provide no passion and no purpose, it costs their companies hundreds of *billions* of dollars lost due to unproductivity, illness, lack of quality and customer service and therefore lost customers, and a myriad of other things. Do you know what it costs individuals like you? It cost your health (it certainly did me), your relationships, your future income, your peace of mind. That is a high price to pay.

What if I told you that it was possible to find your true passion and to live the life you came to live? Would you believe me? Well it's true. And I am living proof. And what if I told you that once you *are* living a life of passion, your whole life changes? Your health improves, you lose weight (if you need to), your relationships improve, people are dying to be around you and to work with you. Your whole outlook on life changes. Just like that.

I know what you are thinking now:

- But what if it doesn't work for me?
- But what if I am the *one* person it doesn't work on?
- But what if I am too scared to face my challenges?
- But what if it is too hard?
- But what if I can't finish?

Guess what? *Everyone* has those fears. Remember the first time you jumped off the diving board or went swimming? Weren't you afraid? But you did it anyway. And you are still here.

Finding your true passion is an archaeological process. You have to do some digging! And digging is scary. But just imagine the buried treasure that you are going to find. Just imagine. I'm *so* excited for you to be at the beginning of this amazing journey you are about to embark on!

CHAPTER 2

My Journey to Passion

*"We must be willing to let go of the life we planned
so as to have the life that is waiting for us."*
–Joseph Campbell

For most of my life, I have been afraid of my true passion. My parents never knew or cared about my interests or desires. My dad was a raging and controlling narcissist and my mother tried to live her life through me. My brother was abusive; my sister was a jealous bully. Being my authentic, true, and individual self was not allowed. Expressing my true passion meant being abused. Every time I tried to shine, I suffered. A lot.

Fast-forward to college, where I changed my major four times before deciding on journalism. I was smart and really good at many things but picking something specific that I really wanted to pursue was *really* hard for me.

After graduating, I got a corporate high-tech job in learning and development, but after a few years, I was bored to death. I had been promoted to the point where there was nowhere else to go (except my boss's job, and that was never going to happen). It was the mid-90s and the internet was happening—I decided I wanted to work for the coolest Web design company in San Francisco, Vivid Studios. I still did not know what my passion was, but I knew I needed to move. That was when I realized what a powerful manifester I was. I decided on the *one* company and the *one* person I wanted to work for. It was an impossible thing that my mind knew I would never get. Everyone wanted to work for Vivid at that time. So I meditated on that job (that within a year, I would be living in San Francisco, working at Vivid Studios, and working with Nathan Shedroff, founder and creative director of Vivid and "boy wonder" of the internet). A few months after that, I went on a trip to San Francisco with a friend of mine, and she asked me why I hadn't moved there yet, as the city suited me perfectly. At the time, my dear aunt was really sick. I could never leave while she was sick, and I didn't have enough money in savings. She asked, "What would it take for you to move here?" I said, "My aunt would have to not be sick anymore, and I would need another $10,000 in savings." The next week, my aunt died and left me $10,000. That really freaked me out. Shortly after that, I attended a conference in San Francisco. I had forgotten to bring my glasses, so I had to sit in the front row. And lo and behold, I was sitting right in front of Nathan Shedroff, of Vivid Studios! We ended up physically running into each other on the break and started talking. We set up an interview, but I didn't get the job. The job I interviewed for was not the right fit. But I ended up moving to San Francisco anyway (with no job). After about a month or so, Nathan called again and asked if I would come back and interview to be the director of the Experience Group. And that is the job I got.

I loved the job at first, and I was good at it. I loved managing people and people loved working for me, but I needed something more. So I left to start my own business managing internet projects virtually, thinking it was just temporary. But then so many companies came to me to help them staff their start-ups that I found a partner and hired employees. We became this really cool boutique staffing agency that handled creative and technical talent for internet start-ups as well as *Fortune* 500 companies. The part I loved the most was helping the talent figure out the right fit for them. But we grew too fast, and it really wasn't my passion—it was my business partner's passion. After the internet bust in 2001, I closed the business and came back to Texas, where I grew up, and back to the corporate world because I knew I could make money. By this time I knew my passion was writing and helping people, but nothing more beyond that. I was too scared to pursue something that would not bring good money right away. So I spent the next several years a corporate zombie. By 2008, I worked for a giant telecom in Dallas, and I was completely miserable, working for a rigid, demanding boss, doing work that was completely unfulfilling. I kept asking myself, "You are so smart and have so many talents. Why are you not pursuing them?" The answer that kept coming back to me was "Because that would not be safe and secure"—as if it was my father answering back! I really wanted to make a difference, to help people and make the world a better place. But what could that be? I had been interested in alternative health for many years. But what could I do? What really jazzed me? What gave me life? Then I remembered back in 1997 when I was living in San Francisco and I attended the Body and Soul conference. I went to a session about healing with Dr. Barbara Brennan and Dr. Bernie Seigel, and it completely blew me away. They were talking about how much power we all have, inside of us, to heal ourselves. I'm not talking Louise Hay's *You Can Heal Your Life* kind of power. I am talking energetic power we all have. It was so fascinating and I remember immediately wanting to sign up for Barbara Brennan's energy healing school in New York. I investigated, but it was not feasible for me at the time. I would have had to move to New York and go to school full time. There was no way I could do that. That was definitely "not safe" for me.

So in 2008 I started to google "energy healing schools." By this time, there were a few more in addition to Barbara Brennan's. Then I discovered the Lionheart Institute in San Antonio, Texas. I could drive there, and it was led and taught by former teachers and deans of Brennan's school. Wow! I immediately called them and found out they held classes once a month on the weekends and were starting a new class in a couple of weeks. It could not have been more perfect!

During my three-year intense program at Lionheart I learned characterology, the study of the five character structures, originated by Austrian psychoanalyst Wilhelm Reich in the 1930s. Since then, I have never been the same. Characterology completely changed my perspective on life and everyone around me. Finally, everything about myself and everyone I knew made complete sense.

The five character structures are sets of patterns formed in response to trauma at different stages of development, starting in utero up to seven or eight years of age. Each structure forms at a different stage of development. The patterns are defense strategies or tendencies that influence body shape, physical and personality traits, beliefs, thoughts, emotions, behaviors, talents, gifts, issues, and challenges. This fascinated me more than anything I had ever learned. And during my study of characterology, I went through the most intense healing I had ever gone through. It was like the "dark night of the soul," as we had to heal all of our structures in the class. It was very challenging, and quite a few people dropped out because they were not ready to face their demons. I had been in traditional counseling (talk therapy) for well over a decade, and it had not made that much of a difference. But characterology? All the difference in the world. I was a completely different person. I lost weight, started seeing an amazing man, started having fun again, dressing differently, and dipping my foot into things like standup comedy. I was completely comfortable in my own skin, something I had not been in a long time or maybe ever. My regular psychotherapist got upset with me and started criticizing both me and Lionheart. So I fired her! Lionheart had taught me that somatic or body-based therapies (like characterology and bioenergetics) were at least ten times more effective than any counseling I had had before. I was not about go backward!

Once I graduated from Lionheart, I started my mind-body practice (on the side, of course—you know, because it was not a secure job). I even got my teacher training certification and co-taught several trainings. In my practice, I did hands-on energy work as well as coaching and counseling. When I used characterology on my clients, it seemed to work so well. Every one of them was fascinated by how much I seemed to know about them during our first meetings. All of a sudden I had X-ray vision to just about everyone I met. I could look at someone and know a hundred things about them because I had learned characterology. It was cool but also a bit unnerving—to have this knowledge. My clients would ask me, "Where can I find out more about this?" or, "Is there a book on this?" At the time there were only large tomes that were written for therapists or healers, but nothing for the normal person. I said to myself back then, "I need to write a book on this."

So I continued on this path as a mind-body coach and practitioner while still keeping my corporate day job at a global software company. I was still afraid to go for it. But I didn't really know what "it" was. Not specifically. I knew I wanted something big, much bigger than being just a mind-body coach on the side. My entire professional career had been in corporate learning and development. I had been an instructional designer, designing large programs, both in person and online; a learning strategist; and a talent/career development expert and coach. I was really good at helping others figure out and pursue what they wanted. But I was still playing it safe. And during this time, I met a personal trainer in Dallas who changed my life. At this point, I was back in full corporate mode and was overworked, exhausted, unmotivated, and overweight, with health problems. He kept telling me, "Until you live a life of passion, nothing is going to change much." At this point, I was somewhat clear about my passion, and I wrote it down. But I had no idea how it was going to "just happen," so I did not move on it.

Then I decided to move to New York City and signed up for Mama Gena's School of Womanly Arts Mastery Program. It was another program that changed my life. I learned so much about desire and cultivating a desire practice. I learned how important and powerful it was to have sisterhood and a real community where you could be completely yourself, with no pretense. I started getting much closer to my true passion and I could feel it bubbling up in me. I knew I needed to write a book and design and run a program having to do with characterology. But how? I couldn't just quit my job and do it. And this stuff is a bit complicated. But if anyone could do it, I could. I am a writer (I have a degree in journalism), learning program designer, and a former business owner and entrepreneur. But how would I make this consumable for the average person? It was a bit daunting, so I put it to the side, as usual.

Meanwhile I was so unhappy and overworked in my corporate job that I got sick. Like, really sick. I was diagnosed with stage 4 adrenal fatigue, which is close to death. I knew I had to do something different or I was going to die. I took some time off work to heal. And then I signed up for yet another program, called "Foundations of Power," with Kasia Urbaniak. Well, this provided the final piece of the puzzle for me.

Kasia is one of the most brilliant and engaging persons I have ever met. In her four-month course, I learned how to truly tune into and hone the true desires within me. And to get *very* specific. How unbelievably powerful that is! It is truly like magic. Once I got clear on my true desires, I came up with what I call my "passion statement" that incorporated my talents, my interests, and my desires, and then I "broadcasted my signal," as Kasia says.

Because I was in tune with my true desires and my true passion, I was in the flow and things just started happening *very* quickly for me. That is when I refined the Come Alive process, completed the Come Alive book and companion program, and quit my corporate job. Immediately afterward people and money started flowing to me. It was just so easy once I made the decision, based solely on my true passion.

Now, not everyone who has taken Mama Gena's Mastery or Kasia's Foundations had the same result as I did. Everyone is in a different place on their journey. But I believe that because I did the characterology work years before, it allowed the other work to come through clean—not muddled by the trauma of my past. I had tackled a lot of my challenges and cleared most of my demons. I honestly believe that when you have not really acknowledged your real issues and challenges, figured out where they came from, and either healed them or transformed them, it is really hard to truly find and live your passion. Before Lionheart, my desires were being squashed and sabotaged by my "inner supervillain." I knew some of my desires, but my challenges prevented me from making them happen.

I have spent years trying to figure this all out. And now that I have, I want to shout it from the rooftops! I want to share it with everyone on the planet. But for now, I am sharing it with you.

It certainly won't take you the twenty years that it took me to get to this place because I am here to guide you every step of the way. I have taken my journey and experience and created a simple process for you to go through. No matter where you are in your passion journey, you will get something out of this book. Whether you are just a reader or a participant in the Come Alive program, this book is meant to be read, worked through and used as a reference over and over. Shall we begin?

CHAPTER 3

The Come Alive Process and Tools

*"We're not on our journey to save the world but to save
ourselves. But in doing that you save the world.
The influence of a vital person vitalizes."*
–Joseph Campbell

The *Come Alive Process* combines my career development work with the mind-body coaching work I have been doing for years. Once I got crystal clear on my own true desires, it hit me like a bolt of lightning. It is a unique process, unlike any you will have experienced. It is challenging, deep, and life-altering. It is also engaging and super fun! It has been super successful with my clients in helping them find and live their passions, and I hope it will be for you, too.

I call my process *Come Alive* because I truly believe all the answers you seek are inside of you, waiting to "come alive." Here is an overview of the Come Alive process, which I will cover step by step in the next several chapters.

THE COME ALIVE PROCESS

1. **Assess Yourself**—You can't go anywhere until you take stock. In this step, you will discover where you are in your life, what brings you joy, and what your dominant archetypes are. This includes an archetype quiz.

2. **Explore Your Archetypes**—Now comes the exploration! This is where you go in deep and investigate your dominant archetypes. You will get a better understanding of your natural traits and tendencies, your gifts and talents, and your challenges and why you have them.

3. **Tackle Your Challenges**—It is my belief that you cannot attain your true purpose and passion until you have repaired some of the damage from the trauma of your past. This is the step where you will identify, accept, and tackle the biggest challenges in your life and where they came from (core beliefs). From there, you

can decide to heal them or transform them to support the life you want. This step can be quite difficult and may take time. To make it a bit less challenging (and actually fun), you will create your own inner supervillain to support you in this step.

4. **Restore Your Brilliance**—Once you have repaired some of the damage, you are ready for restoration! It is amazing what happens after repairs—your whole world changes and all your brilliance starts to rise up. In this step, you will identify and accept your true talents and "superpowers" and learn how to nurture them in order to reclaim your true passion, your true desires. In this step, you will create your own inner superhero to support you.

5. **Hone Your True Desires**—You do not have a choice about your true desires. They reside in your body and have always been there, buried beneath the muck of damage. You may not have known how to connect with them. Now that you have both your inner supervillain and superhero supporting you, you are finally ready to tune into both of them and your body to identify, ignite, and hone your true desires—to come *fully* alive!

6. **Manifest Your Passion**—The final step is manifestation. Now you are ready to write your Passion State-

ment, build a success profile, build or update your personal brand, make a plan of action, and go for it!

HOW TO GET THE MOST OUT OF THIS BOOK

Your Come Alive Journal and Pens

I suggest you get a special notebook to journal and make notes throughout this journey. You will be using it to do the activities throughout the process. I also find it helpful to use a special pen to write with. And if you like to draw or doodle, get some cool, colored pens or pencils.

Partner, Circles, or Groups

This book and process can bring up some tough emotions for a lot of people. You need a support system. If you're not in the Come Alive program, make sure you've got a partner or a buddy to either go through this with you or just have a trusted friend volunteer to be your support system. Some folks form a book club or a circle or even a private or secret Facebook group. Or you can join the Come Alive Facebook group to share and to see other passion seekers' experiences. Everything in the group is completely confidential. I think it is important to be witnessed and supported as you go through the process as it helps you to be accountable through your own journey to your true purpose and passion. I also think it is a good idea to take a picture of yourself at the beginning of this journey and share it with your partner, circle or the Facebook group. Then take another one at the end and compare the two. See how you have changed. You may lose weight (if you need to), you may look younger (finding and living your passion does that to you!), or you may just have a sparkle in your eyes that was not there before. Anything is possible!

YOUR TOOLBOX: ACTIVITIES AND SELF-CARE PRACTICES

I have included many activities and practices throughout this book, but here is one that you can do on a regular basis. I share this here because it is a great one to do first thing in the morning, every morning. It really helps ground you for the day.

Activity—The Three-Body Check-In
(Time required 10–15 minutes)

I am a big proponent of meditation. The quality of my life is directly tied to how often I meditate. I have a few different types of meditation I do regularly, but the one I do most regularly is the three-body check-in. As an energy worker, I check-in with my three different "bodies"—that is, the physical body, the emotional body, and the mental body. This check-in really helps calm and clear my body, emotions, and mind for the day. This check-in is a combination meditation and writing exercise and goes something like this:

1. Sit comfortably in a chair with your back straight, feet on the floor, and a pen and paper or journal close by. You may want to use headphones to listen to meditative music.

2. Close your eyes and notice your breath. If it is shallow, try to deepen it. If it is fast, try to slow it down. Do this until you feel your breath start to regulate.

3. Then start the check-in with your *physical body*. Begin with your feet and do a slow upward scan of your body, noticing anything that is off or needs attention. Write down any sensations or anything of concern. Once done, thank your physical body for serving you today.

4. Move on to your emotions, or *the emotional body*. Again, notice your breath and regulate it as best you can. With eyes closed, ask yourself how you are feeling emotionally. Are you sad, angry, frustrated, joyful? Write down whatever emotions are present for you. You can write something like, "Today, I am feeling _____." Once done, thank your emotions for serving and protecting you today.

5. Move on to the mind, or *the mental body*. Once more notice your breath and regulate it as best you can. Ask yourself, what recurring thoughts or beliefs are popping up today? Write them down. Once done, thank your mind and your beliefs for serving and protecting you today.

6. End with an overall gratitude to all three. Write down at least one thing you are grateful for today.

Tool—Self-Care Inventory

I believe it is vital to have a self-care practice. I have included many self-care practices, tools, and activities in this book and program. I suggest creating a self-care practice inventory in your journal, making note of the practices that you really resonated with and can use on a regular basis. Mine is organized by the following categories:

- Personal self-care (for things like taking a bath, getting a massage, etc.)
- Tools and solo activities (activities I can do alone)
- Partner activities (activities in which I need a partner)
- Movement and sports
- Therapies (suggested therapies or practices in which I need a practitioner)

Toolkit

Most of the tools and activities in the book can be found in the toolkit on our website here: http://comealiveinstitute.com/toolkit. Some of the activities here are inspired by my experiences with Lionheart, Mama Gena, and Kasia Urbaniak, as well as many other programs I have taken.

Okay, it is time to begin the process. Are you ready? The next chapter is the first step: Assess Yourself.

CHAPTER 4

Step One: Assess Yourself

"The privilege of a lifetime is being who you are."
–Joseph Campbell

THE SELF-CARE WHEEL

Are you ready to start the journey? Let's first discover *where* you are in your life. A snapshot, if you will. If you've ever worked with a coach before, you are most likely familiar with the Wheel of Life. My wheel is a bit different—it is completely focused on self-care. If you picked up this book, you are most likely lacking in self-care. Heck, most people are lacking in self-care! The Self-Care Wheel includes categories that I think are vital to living a happy and fulfilling life. A life of passion. Even though your passion/purpose is only one spoke of the wheel, finding it affects all other spokes. It is really important to see where you are on all spokes at the beginning of this journey—because at the end of this journey, you will see just how far you progress.

Look at the wheel provided and mark where you are or how satisfied you are with the following areas. (You can also download and print a copy of the wheel to mark up at http://www. comealiveinstitute.com/toolkit.)

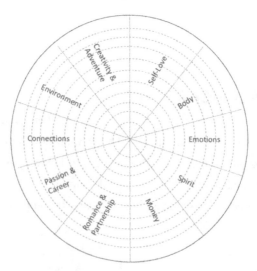

1. **Self-Love**—How well do you love yourself? How much self-confidence do you have right now? How is your motivation to do the things you need or want to do?

2. **Body**—How good is your physical health? How is your nutrition? How well do you sleep? How active are you? Do you have a movement practice?

3. **Emotions**—How is your emotional and behavioral health? Are you emotionally reactive or are you holding your emotions inside? How well do you handle stress?

4. **Spirit**—Do you have a regular prayer or meditation practice? Do you have peace of mind? Do you make time to engage in spiritual practices that fulfill you?

5. **Money**—How satisfied are you with your relationship with money? Do you make what you are worth? Are you planning for your future? Do you have a budget?

6. **Romance and Partnership**—How satisfied are you with your love life? If you have a partner, how satisfied are you with the relationship? How satisfied are you sexually?

7. **Passion and Career**—Do you know what your life purpose or passion is? If so, is that also your career? How satisfied are you with your career? Are you doing what you love?

8. **Connections**—How satisfied are you with your connections in your life? Do you spend quality time with friends

or associates? Do you have a community? Do you actively engage in sisterhood (women) or brotherhood (men)?

9. **Environment**—How satisfied are you with where you live (country, state/province, and city)? Do you live or work near nature? How satisfied are you with your home environment? Does it energize you, bring you peace or joy? How satisfied are you with your work environment? Are you able to get things done?

10. **Creativity and Adventure**—Do you have creative outlets that you engage in regularly? Do you travel for pleasure? How often do you engage in activities that bring you joy? Do you have adventure in your life?

Notice something big missing from this wheel? That's right—*Family*. You know why? Because the *Self*-Care Wheel is all about *you* and how well you are taking care of yourself, not your family.

This exercise can bring up some emotions, so you may want to make some notes in your journal. If you are doing this book with a friend or group, share your wheels and talk about how the wheel was for you to complete. Keep this wheel handy as we will revisit it later in the book.

HAPPY HAPPY JOY JOY

Okay, now let's shift to talking about *what* brings you joy and pleasure. Take out your journal and answer the following questions:

- What interests or activities did you *love* to do as a child or adolescent? Write down at least ten things that brought you joy as a kid. How did your parents or other family members support these interests? Make some notes on this.

- If you could have five different lives, what would they be? Be as outrageous as you want to be! Ballet dancer, archaeologist, opera singer, yoga teacher, movie star—whatever you think would be fascinating or bring you joy, adventure, or pleasure.

- What brings you joy or pleasure now? Write down at least ten things. It can be as simple (eating ice cream) or as complex (climbing a mountain) as you like. Do you do any of those things on a regular basis? If not, why not?

THE FIVE DEVELOPMENTAL ARCHETYPES

Now let's shift to discovering *who* you are. Remember Wilhelm Reich's Five Character Structures I talked about in my journey (Chapter 2)? Over the years, many people have taken Reich's work and modified it in different ways. Well I have modified and simplified his work so that it can easily be used for self-discovery and growth. Instead of character structures, I call them the Five Developmental Archetypes, since that is really what they are—archetypes.

While working with the archetypes, I realized just how valuable they were in helping people discover and understand *who* they are and *why* they are the way they are. In addition, they help guide you in identifying your challenges and obstacles as well as your gifts and talents. It is important to note that we all have *all* five of them, just in different increments. But usually one to three of them are more dominant. And your dominant one may change, depending on how you grow and change.

I will go into each archetype in detail in the next chapter. For now, let's take a quiz to see which archetypes are dominant for you. In this quiz, I am only grouping them by numbers (not their names), so as not to skew the results.

Review the groupings of statements below and put a check by each one that is true for you. Then add up how many checks you have for each archetype. The ones with the most checks will be your dominant archetypes. Most people have two or three dominant archetypes. Some of these statements may sound odd, but they help determine your dominant archetype(s). Just go with it! Please be completely honest. This is *only* for you to see (no one else). If you prefer not marking up this book, you can find a copy of the quiz to download or print here: http://www.comealiveinstitute.com/toolkit.

ARCHETYPE QUIZ

Archetype 1

__ I love spending time alone.

__ For most of my life, I have been thin and have had a hard time gaining weight.

__ I have a problem with anxiety or worry.

__ I am fiercely independent and prefer working alone.

__ I am easily distracted and have a hard time focusing on one thing for long.

__ I am uncomfortable or a bit awkward in social situations.

__ I love animals and often prefer being with them more than people.

__ I love spending time in nature and would rather be there than with people.

__ I am gifted artistically (music, singing, performing, fine art, etc.).

__ I am intellectual and nerdy (like math, science, sci-fi, gadgets, high-tech).

__ I am a creative, innovative, and visionary thinker but have a hard time seeing things through to fruition.

__ I do not make the kind of money I should (don't charge enough for services, work in a job that is beneath my skill set, do not get paid for my real talents, etc.).

___ I am in my head a lot and sometimes have a hard time connecting with others.

___ Being in a relationship is not that important to me.

___ I am very uncomfortable being the center of attention.

Total ___

Archetype 2

___ I do not like being alone.

___ I have almost always been in a long-term relationship (rarely without a partner).

___ My upper body is smaller than my lower body (shoulders narrower than hips).

___ It is important for me to be heard and "talk things out" with my partner, boss or coworker.

___ I have a gift with words, both writing and speaking.

___ I am very generous and love buying gifts for others.

___ I love to share information and would make a great teacher.

___ People have told me that I am very charming.

___ I prefer collaboration and working with others rather than working alone.

___ Sometimes I feel like my needs are never going to be met.

___ I never feel like I have enough (money, love, etc.).

___ I need validation from others (boss, coworker, partner).

___ I like when attention is on me.

__ I don't really know what I want and don't have many interests or hobbies outside work or home.

__ I have (or have had) issues with addictions (cigarettes, alcohol, food, shopping or sex).

Total ___

Archetype 3

__ I have or have had weight problems in my life (thirty or more pounds overweight).

__ I have tendency to over-give, both at home and at work.

__ I am hardworking and responsible.

__ I have a tendency to rescue others.

__ I am compassionate and empathetic and have a gift for helping others.

__ I am afraid to show the "real me" to others, as they may not like me, be scared, etc.

__ I can easily adapt to any situation at work or at home.

__ Sometimes I feel like I am either not enough or too much.

__ I am highly intuitive and can easily take on other people's energy or emotions.

__ I do not speak up for myself like I should and have hard time saying "no" and setting boundaries with others (partners, family, boss, etc.).

__ I hold in my anger and am afraid to let it out.

__ I sometimes resent others who seem to have it "so easy" and ask myself, "When is it going to be *my* turn?"

__ I feel like it is more important to please others than fulfill my own needs.

__ I am very sensitive and am crushed by criticism.

__ I do not like attention on myself and have a hard time being seen and "putting myself out there."

Total ___

Archetype 4

__ I am a good leader.

__ My upper body is larger than my lower body (chest/shoulders wider than hips).

__ I am very confident in my abilities.

__ I am visionary and entrepreneurial.

__ I am a "take charge" kind of person.

__ I do not like being wrong and will go to lengths to prove "I am right."

__ I like to lead every project I am on and have a hard time letting someone else lead.

__ I am brave, spontaneous, and willing to take risks.

__ I inspire others to go for what they want.

__ I am comfortable on a stage, speaking in front of crowds.

__ I am very generous to those who are loyal to me.

__ I make things happen.

__ I like to be the "smartest person in the room."

__ I like giving orders and being in control of situations.

__ I hate to admit this, but when someone crosses me, I want to retaliate in some way.

Total ___

Archetype 5

__ I have never had a weight problem, my body is well-proportioned and I have almost always been lean and fit.

__ Appearances are very important to me. I always try to look as perfect as I can.

__ I aim for perfection in everything that I do.

__ I have very healthy boundaries and do not have a problem saying "no" to others.

__ I am fair and balanced and try to operate from integrity at all times.

__ I have a fear of losing control, so I keep my emotions in check at all times.

__ I have a hard time being spontaneous and do not like to change plans.

__ My house is always neat and put together.

__ I am highly competitive.

__ I have never missed a deadline.

__ I am a high achiever and take pride in my accomplishments.

__ I am ambitious and driven and make a good, fair leader.

__ I am afraid of my feelings sometimes, so I just push them down.

__ People have told me that I can seem cold and unfeeling.

__ I have a hard time being vulnerable.

Total ___

THE RESULTS

The 5 archetypes are listed below. Write down your totals for each one:

1. The Dreamer ____
2. The Charmer ____
3. The Endurer ____
4. The Commander ____
5. The Achiever ____

So which archetype had the most checks? Are you a combination of two or more types? Anything over 10 checks is a dominant archetype, but the one that has the most checks will be your dominant for sure. I am a combination of three myself (1, 3, and 5—dreamer, endurer, and commander). Are you curious about what this means? Let's move on to the next chapter to explore your dominant archetype(s) in more detail.

CHAPTER 5

Step Two:
Explore Your Archetypes

"*The cave you fear to enter holds the treasure you seek.*"
–Joseph Campbell

I n this chapter we are going to explore the Five Developmental Archetypes in more detail. I would encourage you to read about all of them and not just your dominant ones, as you may gain more insight into yourself as well as others in your life. Each archetype has specific traits, tendencies, beliefs, thoughts, emotions, gifts, talents, and challenges. You will certainly not have *all* of the characteristics of your dominant archetypes, but you will have many of them. The purpose of this is to gain insight into yourself, understand a bit more about why you are the way you are, and really acknowledge your true gifts as well as your challenges.

MIRROR MIRROR

This is the step where you look at and own your stuff! Good or bad. This step can be a bit scary or make you super uncomfortable. I know when I first learned about the archetypes, it was hard to acknowledge that I had some of these traits, especially the negative ones. But once I took it all in, I took this big sigh of relief and said, "Oh, *that's* why I do that" and, "No wonder that has been so hard for me most of my life." It gave me such a sense of freedom in my life and really helped me to stop blaming or shaming myself for certain things. I hope it does for you as well. Speaking of blaming—discovering your archetypes and where they came from (trauma at certain stages of life) is not an excuse to blame your parents, caregivers, or others for something that happened to you. We are all human and have suffered trauma as a result. And by trauma, I mean anything that your "child self" experienced or perceived as dangerous or harmful. I truly believe that all parents and caregivers do their best, given their circumstances. And I personally am grateful that I have the archetypes I have because without that trauma, I would not be the *amazing* person I am today.

In this book, I am covering the basics of each archetype as it applies to finding your passion. Each section below covers an archetype. Each archetype's section starts with a general overview or story of that type and then list details and ends with some fun celebrity and fictional examples. As you go through these, try to identify what applies to you. Keep in mind that we will go into solutions to the challenges and issues in the next chapter.

A little note about the physical traits associated with each archetype. You do not have to have these in order to be considered that as your dominant type, but if you *do* possess the physical traits, then you are *definitely* that type. And the more work you do on yourself (to heal), the more the negative traits will diminish, even the physical ones.

One more note, I use the pronoun she throughout the descriptions since I mainly work with women. If you are a male or identify as male, please contact me at info@comealiveinstitute.com as I want to know how many men are interested in my work!

Okay, let's take a deep breath and dive into the archetypes!

THE DREAMER

The dreamer is the first archetype to form in the body, forming in utero to six months old. The dreamer suffered a trauma at this stage that created a sense of terror in the body and formed the archetype. She is fearful of the real world and would much rather be in the spiritual world or in her head. She does not have a real sense of her physical self because her energy does not fully occupy her body most of the time—her energy is mostly in her head and above her head.

The dreamer is extremely intellectual and visionary and may be artistically inclined. Since the physical world is not a safe place, she suffers from anxiety and spends a lot of time in her head, fantasizing, creating, and dreaming of other places that are safer than "being here now." She may have a hard time connecting in person with others and is more comfortable engaging through devices, social media, etc.

The dreamer is a creative wonder, coming up with many ideas and solutions to problems. Sometimes she has so many ideas that she doesn't know what to do with them all. She is much more comfortable working alone than collaborating with others. Because of the constant presence of fear in the body, she suffers from anxiety and may drink alcohol or take anti-anxiety medication just to feel "normal."

Socializing or going to a party and interacting with lots of people is the dreamer's nightmare. If the dreamer goes to a party, she will spend most of her time alone and leave early. She would much rather stay home with her cat and read a book. When her anxiety gets the better of her, she may suffer panic attacks. The dreamer's greatest fear is also her greatest desire—to connect with others and feel like she matters and that she truly belongs.

The Dreamer—General Info and Physical Traits

- Developmental Stage—in utero to six months old
- Energy—ungrounded, withdrawing, leaving, up and out
- Possible physical traits—usually thin or very thin (could have been very thin growing up), tall with a long neck, large forehead with big eyes, small wrists and ankles, feet have high arches
- Possible physical challenges—spinal issues (scoliosis), joint issues (energetic leakages), lack of coordination/ balance issues, anorexia or trouble gaining weight (from energy not being down in her body), stress and adrenal issues, gut issues (from stress and anxiety)

The Dreamer—Personality Traits, Talents, and Gifts

- Brilliant, highly intellectual, deep thinker
- Strong imagination, dreams *big*, visionary, extremely creative
- Creative genius "gift from god"

- Artistically gifted or inclined (music, fine art, acting, dancing, filmmaking, writing, etc.)
- Highly independent
- Highly spiritual—connects to God/spirit/universe easily
- Highly intuitive/clairvoyant/psychic—may be able to communicate with the "other side"
- Huge animal and nature lover

The Dreamer—Emotions/Tendencies

- Core Emotion—fear (constant fear is always present in body)
- Common Negative Emotions—strong anxiety and worry, disconnected, detached, hypervigilant, always assumes rejection
- Common Tendencies—scattered; short attention span; spacey (head in the clouds); gravitates toward individual sports; house/desk may be chaotic and messy; can appear smart and intellectual one minute and very spacey and forgetful the next; favors animals, art, or solitary activity over people
- Possible challenges—social anxiety, panic attacks, insomnia, paranoia, or obsessive thoughts (in head all the time); all roads lead to "I don't matter"; hysteria/"freaking out"; phobias (like agoraphobia); sui-

cidal thoughts when feeling very stressed, triggered, or unsafe

- Possible addictions—alcohol or antianxiety medication to feel "normal" or to be able to connect to others, sleep meds for insomnia, possible opioid addiction for intense anxiety/pain

The Dreamer—Defensive Behaviors

- Spacing out, daydreaming (loves hanging out in "spirit-land"), overwhelmed, distracted behavior, procrastination
- Forgetfulness, losing things, getting lost easily (not good with directions or maps)
- Freezing, being quiet/not speaking up, disappearing / "ghosting," isolation
- Intellectualization, showing intellectual superiority
- Hurried behavior/speech, spurts of energy followed by exhaustion
- Other people may perceive her behavior as aloof, snobby, rude, cold, unfeeling, delusional, strange, odd, antisocial

The Dreamer—Negative Thoughts/Statements/Beliefs

- Thoughts/statements—I don't want to be here, I want to disappear or escape, I don't matter, I can do it myself,

I don't need anyone, leave me alone, I don't belong, don't look at me, I'm leaving, it is dangerous/scary to be present in my body, I am above this, my inner world is special and more important than mundane worldly interactions with people

- Possible negative beliefs—people are not safe; connecting with others is dangerous; being seen is dangerous; hiding is good; it is safer to be alone; if I am seen, then I could be hurt; being shut down is safe; if I operate from my light, then I am a target for abuse, betrayal, harm, annulation, or death

The Dreamer—In Relationships

- Would rather be alone than with others
- Being in a relationship/partnership is not important
- May never marry or have children
- Has sex to feel alive
- Possible relationship challenges—has difficulty being truly intimate with another person and sustaining a long-term romantic relationship, tends to "ghost" relationships, will leave or reject a partner before she is rejected, more comfortable with long-distance relationships or just being alone

The Dreamer—At Work/School

- Prefers to work alone and/or virtually (if possible)
- Creative, innovative, and visionary thinker—the *idea* person
- Prefers ideation to execution
- Devises creative, innovative solutions to *big* problems
- Possible challenges—has a difficult time asking for help; gets easily distracted; has a hard time finishing projects on time or seeing things through to the end; does not like to present in front of others, be called out, or be in the spotlight (creates a lot of anxiety)

The Dreamer—Examples from Music, Film, TV, etc.

- Luna Lovegood (from *Harry Potter*)
- Prince (+Achiever)
- Michael Jackson (+Achiever)
- Lorde
- Amy Winehouse
- Sia Furler
- Sheldon (from *Big Bang Theory*)
- Sherlock (from PBS's *Sherlock*)
- Scarecrow (from *Wizard of Oz*)
- Donkey (from *Shrek*)

THE CHARMER

The charmer archetype forms in the breast-feeding stage (three to twenty-four months). The charmer did not get the attention she needed at this stage, which created a sense of deprivation and abandonment, and, therefore, she is terrified of being alone. Because she never felt like she got enough nourishment, time, and attention, she is always seeking attention from others (both in her personal and professional life). She is very clever and has learned how to get attention from others. She can be a shameless self-promoter if she wants. She has learned how to be charming, persuasive, and even manipulative to get what she wants. But nothing ever seems enough. She never feels like she has enough love, attention, or money (no matter how much she has). She can drive her partners, bosses, or coworkers crazy with the constant need for validation or attention. She can be a very demanding mom or boss or a very generous one (or can go back and forth). On the flip side, the charmer is very loving and extremely generous and loves giving gifts. She has an amazing gift with words, is great at presenting her ideas, and is great with people and the public. The charmer can be very emotional and can cry or get angry very easily, especially when she does not get what she wants. The charmer's greatest fear is abandonment and her greatest desire is unconditional love.

The Charmer—General Info and Physical Traits

- Energy –pulling, sucking, vampire-like

- Developmental Stage—three months to two years (breast-feeding stage)
- Possible physical traits—upper body is smaller than lower body (or was as an adolescent), may be pear shaped (if overweight), shoulders may be small and sunken, puppy dog eyes that pull you in like a vacuum cleaner, long neck with head tilted forward and chin jutting out
- Possible physical challenges—weakness in upper body, shoulder and neck issues, exhaustion, breast issues (breast cancer), shallow breathing

The Charmer—Personality Traits, Talents, and Gifts
- Nurturing and loving
- Extremely generous, loves giving gifts
- Gifted communicator—ability to write, perform, speak and share
- Very charming, very good at getting what she wants
- Very persuasive, can draw anyone into a conversation
- Great ability with people
- Ability to help others feel loved
- Natural teacher—loves to share information

The Charmer—Emotions/Tendencies
- Core Emotion—sadness, grief

- Common Negative Emotions—needy, powerless, weak, tired, empty, hopeless, lost, lonely, jealous, envious, terrified of being alone, rejection or abandonment
- Common Tendencies—finds it hard to state needs, always feels deprived, an inner emptiness that cannot be filled, deep shame of having needs, uses charm and sexual attraction to get what she wants, overwhelming need to "be heard," shows affection by giving gifts to others, loves attention, loves to talk, seeks fame and notoriety (needs to be the star of any event, party, etc.), deep belief that no one is there to fulfill her needs
- Possible challenges—extreme emotions (anger, sadness), feelings of desperation, lashing out at others for no apparent reason, moodiness, constant feelings of never having enough (love, money, etc.)
- Possible addictions—addictive personality, substance abuse (usually cigarettes or alcohol), eating disorders (bulimia, overeating), excessive shopping, sex addiction

The Charmer—Defensive Behaviors

- Communicates with emotions, very emotional, can fall apart easily
- Neediness, victimization ("poor me"), whininess, codependence

- Overwhelming feelings of need countered with "I don't need" (back and forth)
- Makes demands of others, expects others to take care of her needs (without expressing those needs)
- Drama—acting out to get attention, overreacting to perceived abandonment
- Manipulation, blaming others for problems
- Projects own behavior onto others (only way to look at her behavior is to "see" it in someone else)
- Excessive talking—talking is a way to avoid feeling her own emptiness
- Clinginess, holding on, not being able to leave, panic at being alone
- Other people may perceive behavior as: too chatty, selfish, greedy, "bottomless pit of need," helpless, nagging

The Charmer—Negative Thoughts/Statements/ Beliefs

- Thoughts/statements—I can't do it alone, you owe it to me, you need to do this for me, I don't have needs, my needs are not okay, nothing is wrong with me, you should know what I want, I'll leave you before you leave me, you're so selfish, you suck, I'm fine, I will never be enough, I need your energy in order to survive, I will never get what I want, in the end you will leave me, I won't ask for what I want because I won't get it anyway, you should love me unconditionally

- Possible negative beliefs—I am not worthy enough for someone else to be there; if I need, I will be abandoned; if I am strong, I will be abandoned; if this person goes away (abandons me), I lose my power; there will never be a time when my needs are met

The Charmer—In Relationships

- Being in a relationship is very important
- Is almost always in a relationship (rarely goes without having a partner)
- Strong need for sex (to feel connection with another person)
- Possible relationship challenges—will stay in a horrible relationship just to have someone there (terrified of being alone), will not break up with someone until she has someone else waiting and ready to jump into another relationship, struggles with being alone (even for one night), needs frequent validation from partner (partner can never give her enough), does not do well with long-distance relationships (need someone physically there), will give love to get love, likes receiving and not giving in a relationship, may pursue partners who are unavailable to re-create abandonment

The Charmer—At Work/School

- Great at marketing and sales
- Very persuasive—can sell just about anything
- Prefers collaboration as opposed to working alone
- Great at presentations and performance (on stage, in front of others)
- Great at working with the public
- Possible challenges—needs frequent validation and positive feedback from boss and coworkers, not great at listening to others (focus is mostly on self), needs a lot of attention, may have a tendency to get others to do her work for her and take credit for it

The Charmer—Examples from Music, Film, TV, etc.

- Carrie Fisher
- Chandler from *Friends*
- Phillip Seymour Hoffman
- Puss 'n' Boots from *Shrek*
- Kim Kardashian
- Jennifer Lopez (+Achiever)
- Beyoncé (+Achiever)
- Oprah Winfrey (+Endurer)
- Lady Gaga (+Achiever)
- Timothée Chalamet (+Dreamer)

THE ENDURER

The endurer archetype forms in the toddler stage (two to three years). The endurer experienced shame from not being allowed to fully express herself (her emotions, physical expressions, movements, abilities, or interests) or through enmeshment with her mother, where she could not understand the difference between her needs and her mother's needs. Either way, she learned that her needs were not her own and not important. She learned to hold everything *in* because she had been punished if she let out her emotions or fully expressed her toddler self. She learned that her emotions and her expressions were *not* OK and that it was not safe to fully be herself. She eventually learned that she was either too much or not enough. She learned self-abandonment through outward projection in order to protect herself from abuse by becoming hypervigilant to the feelings of others. For this reason, she has yet to learn how to be in touch with her own feelings and needs. Her self-expression has been bottled up like a pressure cooker. Life has not been about being true to herself but about what others have imposed on her. Often her first self-proclamation is rage; however, underneath that are multifaceted layers and depths of a truly compassionate and sensitive soul. The endurer is always thinking of others and how she can help them. She is always putting herself last because that is what she has always done. Putting herself first is very foreign.

The endurer's greatest fear and her greatest desire are the same—expressing her true self.

The Endurer—General Info and Physical Traits

- Developmental Stage—two to three years old (autonomy stage)
- Energy –holding in and down into self
- Possible physical traits—bigger structure, carrying extra weight (fat or muscle) for protection, holding in thighs, buttocks, and neck—causing neck to get shorter, waist to get shorter, pelvis to tuck in (flat butt)
- Possible physical challenges—stress; tension in neck and shoulders (carrying the weight of the world); problems with constipation (holding in or back); lots of inertia; can suffer from heart issues and high blood pressure, diabetes, weight problems

The Endurer—Personality Traits, Talents, and Gifts

- Empathetic, compassionate
- Has a gift for helping others, especially those who feel victimized
- Kind, warm, loving, big hearted
- Sensitive, highly intuitive, and can easily take on other people's energy or emotions

- Very thoughtful, understanding, always thinking of how to help others
- Very protective of others, rescuing others
- Generous with time and attention
- Very caring, great at being a caregiver
- Hardworking and responsible
- Persistent, will not give up
- Has great endurance—can take on a lot

The Endurer—Emotions/Tendencies

- Core Emotion—anger
- Common Negative Emotions—inner rage, boiling inside, unworthiness, guilt, shame, spite, resentment, seething, self-doubt, no confidence, denial, depleted, exhausted, confusion, numb, heavy, inert, depressed, unmotivated, squashed, weight of the world on shoulders, hopeless, stuck
- Common Tendencies—afraid to show "the real me," has a very hard time setting boundaries, always puts self on back burner, super sensitive to criticism, over-gives to others to avoid own emotions (anger), self-expression is bottled up inside (like a pressure cooker), being "the good girl," detaches from emotions since they are dangerous, goes back and forth

from being "not enough" to "too much," spends most of life feeling powerless, envious of others who seem "to have it all," does not like to be touched *or* is very touchy-feely, holds grudges, does not know how to set healthy boundaries (allows others to take advantage of her)

- Possible challenges—anger can build up over time and then explode and can lead to feeling out of control or "going crazy," did not learn to process emotions effectively as a child and has a problem doing it as an adult
- Possible addictions—food, sugar, watching TV (anything that keeps the inertia), alcohol or pain killers to numb the pain of not expressing her real emotions

The Endurer—Defensive Behaviors

- Strong, friendly, helpful mask
- Sparks anger in someone else so she has an excuse to get mad
- Uses weight to slow down feelings
- Constant complaining
- Passive aggression
- Martyrdom and victimization ("why me?" or "poor me")

- Self-deprecating (easily makes fun of self), uses laughter and humor to mask the pain inside
- Lashes out at someone once she has finally "had enough" (cannot contain her bottled-up anger anymore)
- Other people may perceive behavior as: compliant, sweet, quiet, calm, "going with the flow," *or* the opposite—loud/too much, raging, vengeful

The Endurer—Negative Thoughts/Statements/ Beliefs

- Thoughts/statements—I am *not* this body, I am something deep inside; my body is my defense; I'm fine; I'll do it; I'll take care of it; whatever you want; I'm not mad; it's not your fault, it's my fault; it is not safe to show my anger; I will not show my emotions; I don't even know who I am; self-defeat is the only way to win; I don't get mad, I get even; it is more important to please others than to fulfill my own needs
- Possible negative beliefs—thoughts and feelings of others affect me; if I express my anger, I won't be loved; the body is not safe; pleasure is not to be trusted; if I keep my self deeply hidden inside, no one can hurt me; my impulses are dangerous; my behavior is bad; if I am allowed to assert myself, I will lose

my power and have to surrender; expressing myself is dangerous; if I express who I really am, I will be punished; if I show my anger, I could kill someone (or myself)

The Endurer—In Relationships

- If married, will absorb emotions and problems of family, partner, children
- Takes on the majority of work for the family
- Caregiver of all family members
- Possible relationship challenges—will stay in a loveless marriage because it is her duty, burden, etc.; takes on lots of burdens because she feels she has to in order to survive; holds grudges about petty things in a marriage; resentful of having to do all the work in the family

The Endurer—At Work/School

- Can take on the work of many others
- Very productive
- Can adapt to any work environment
- Needs very little support or supervision (figures stuff out on her own)
- Will sacrifice to make a deadline

- Makes a caring manager or leader, really takes care of/ protects her employees
- Possible challenges—has a tendency to take on too much work and then gets resentful of others for it, habitually doing another person's work (cleaning up after them, rescuing them), will not speak up and set boundaries at work, may get exhausted from taking on too much work

The Endurer—Examples from Music, Film, TV, etc.

- Hagrid in Harry Potter
- Samwise in Lord of the Rings
- Uncle Buck/John Candy
- Shrek
- Milton in Office Space
- Eeyore in Winnie the Pooh
- The Hulk from Marvel (+Commander)
- Popeye
- Walter from The Big Lebowski
- Rosie O'Donnell
- Jack Black
- Melissa McCarthy
- Chris Farley (+Charmer)

THE COMMANDER

The commander archetype forms at around three to four years. The commander experienced a betrayal of the heart caused by being favored by one parent, but only for a limited amount of time. She learned not trust others' motives as a result. She quickly learned that if she was not "special," then she was "wrong," and wrong is bad. She was also treated like an adult when she was child and therefore never got be in touch with her own authenticity. She feels betrayed and has a difficult time trusting anyone. She later realizes that her "specialness" was really due to following someone else's dream for her (her parents'). Because of being "puffed up" by her parents (or one parent), her chest grew larger than her lower body. Many times during her adolescence she took care of her parents (role reversal). She learned that she needed to be in charge of everything and everyone around her and that she could not really depend on anyone else to do it. She has a tendency to be bossy and can lash out at others if she those around her do not respect her authority. On the flip side, she is a charismatic leader who inspires others and may have a devoted following. She is loyal to those who are close to her (both at home and at work). Her biggest fear is "being wrong" about anything and she will go to lengths to prove that she is right about something (even when she knows she is wrong!). Her greatest desire is to be a devoted leader (to her family, business, etc.) and inspire others.

The Commander—General Info and Physical Traits

- Developmental Stage—three to five years old
- Energy—dominant and projecting out
- Possible physical traits—broad shoulders/inflated chest, small pelvis, upper body is bigger than lower body, can be apple-shaped (if overweight), eyes are commanding and controlling, lots of energy in face
- Possible physical challenges—upper body is hyperactive; lower body is weaker and collapsing; weak hips, knees, and feet; upper back problems; heart issues

The Commander—Personality Traits, Talents, and Gifts

- Fearless leader
- Visionary, entrepreneurial
- Courageous, willing to take risks, warrior type
- Confident, charismatic
- Take charge kind of person, likes to be in control, likes to dominate, likes to be responsible and in control of situations
- Makes things happen, encourages others, pushes others to be great
- Devoted, loyal, protective
- Spontaneous, adventurous, passionate
- Expects to be taken care of
- Ability to go-go-go

- Likes to be "right" about everything, insists on getting her way
- Can be very charming and attractive with compelling eyes

The Commander—Destructive Emotions/Tendencies

- Core Emotion—betrayal
- Common Negative Emotions—betrayed, angry, detached, superior, above, powerful, imitated, impatient, incredulous, disgusted, frustrated, exasperated, untouchable, dominant, aggressive, judgmental, impatient
- Common Tendencies—easily wounded pride, master at manipulating others, anything to keep the pretense that she knows everything or "is right," never wrong, "know it all," never admits fault, will blame others, needs to be in control of every relationship, projects needs onto others
- Possible challenges—has a hard time truly trusting others; when feeling disempowered, she can lash out and become very aggressive and combative
- Possible addictions—power, substances that make her feel powerful and in charge, can get addicted to having arguments just to prove she is "right"

The Commander—Defensive Behaviors

- Power mask

- Unforgiving, very hard to apologize or admit fault
- Narcissistic, "better than" mentality
- Untruthfulness, tends to exaggerate own characteristics
- Goes back and forth between grandiosity and worthlessness
- Passive aggression
- Tendency to blame others for her own mistakes
- Other people may perceive behavior as: narcissism, bullying, unbending, aggressive, or combative

The Commander—Negative Thoughts/Statements/Core Beliefs

- Thoughts/statements—I am in control, you will do what I want, I have to be in control to be safe, life is a battle and I have to win, I'm right and you're wrong, I am above and you are below, I have to win, losing is not an option, I'm better than you, I'm in power, I am in charge, my way or the highway, talk to the hand, I'm special, I'm more special than you, you know I'm right, I'm really smarter than you, my idea is the best, what's wrong with you that you don't get it, over my dead body, you don't know what you're talking about, this is war and I am going to win
- Possible negative core beliefs—I have to be right or I'll die; for me to be right, you have to be wrong; I'll hurt you before you hurt me; I have to be in control to

be safe; I was not allowed to individuate into my own person in my own time

The Commander—In Relationships

- If married, has to be "in charge" of relationship or family
- Makes demands of partner and other family members
- Responds well to flattery
- Tends to "become parent" to her own parents
- Possible relationship challenges—has to win every argument, fear of failing as a parent (just as her parents failed her), hard to maintain relationships with others as equals (especially others with dreamer or charmer archetypes)

The Commander—At Work/School

- Deep leadership abilities
- Visionary, confident, courageous
- Take-charge kind of person, gets things done
- Encourages others, rewards loyalty
- Ability to help others self-achieve and manifest
- Inspires others to be great and to go for what she wants
- Will go around obstacles to see her vision to reality
- Very comfortable speaking to groups of people, getting people excited
- Will ask others to sacrifice to make a deadline

- Being seen as successful is very important
- Possible challenges—has to be the "smartest person in the room," has to be in charge of every project she is on and has a hard time letting someone else lead, communicates by dictating to others, tends to get what she wants through manipulation of coworkers or underlings, may avoid/badmouth/seek revenge on those who have exposed her weaknesses

The Commander—Examples from Music, Film, TV, etc.

- The Hulk from Marvel (+ Endurer)
- Thor from Marvel
- Buzz Lightyear from *Toy Story*
- Superman
- Wonder Woman
- Xena, Warrior Princess
- Indiana Jones
- Arnold Schwarzenegger (+Endurer)
- Sylvester Stallone/Rambo
- Hugh Jackman
- Zac Efron
- Justin Timberlake (+ Achiever)
- Taraji P. Henson
- Catherine Zeta-Jones (+Achiever)

THE ACHIEVER

The achiever archetype forms in the puberty stage (six to nine years). The achiever experienced a rejection when a parent (usually opposite sex parent) rewarded "correct" behavior and withdrew when behavior was "incorrect." Certain spontaneous creative impulses were rejected and others rewarded, creating a split. This created a rejection and loss of the achiever's authenticity, her true sense of self, and her sexuality and sensuality. This created a split between head and heart. As a result she learned to cut off her emotions altogether. She learned that showing emotions of any sort showed weakness. She also learned that accomplishments and perfection equated to love. So she strived to make straight As, eat right, exercise regularly, and hold her body tight so that she would not let anything in (or out). She was forced into being an adult at an early age. As she got older, she did everything that her parents wanted her to do. A typical achiever graduated with honors from college, got a great job, married the perfect man, bought a great house, and had two kids. But she may be quite unhappy and does not know why. She knows she is not in touch with her emotions, but she does not know how to get in touch with them. Her greatest fear is being imperfect, and her greatest desire is fairness and balance in all things.

The Achiever—General Info and Physical Traits
- Developmental Stage—six to nine years old (puberty)

- Energy —contained, holding back
- Possible physical traits—lean, fit, well-proportioned, balanced, long neck and torso
- Possible physical challenges—spinal and back issues; back muscles are tight due to use of will to "get it right," hold it in, do perfectly; the constant "keeping up appearances" mode creates a stiff posture with a straight and erect backbone and a head held high

The Achiever—Personality Traits, Talents, and Gifts

- Loves beauty, quality, and perfection
- Has incredible integrity, clarity, and balance
- Determined, ambitious, competitive
- Impeccably dressed
- House is always clean and perfect
- Very accomplished—can be good at everything she does
- Has high morality and values
- Great with boundaries
- Very organized and cannot tolerate chaos
- Loves routines—uncomfortable being spontaneous, changing plans
- Acts appropriately rather than authentically
- Very controlling of herself, her emotions, and her environment

The Achiever—Negative Emotions/Tendencies

- Core Emotion—*no* emotions (feeling like she has no emotions)
- Common Negative Emotions—most emotions are fake; will not show emotions, does not show anger, emotions show weakness, extreme fear of intense feelings, never feels like she is enough, fear of showing essential self and of feeling truly alive, has "body armor," no flow of emotions in body
- Common Tendencies—equates approval with love; strong fear of intimacy; extremely self-conscious; when she connects, she feels vulnerable; sets up a pattern to achieve, achieve, achieve; needs acknowledgment of accomplishments; doesn't let feelings in or out; maintains a surface of perfection; longs for love yet may not know how to feel this longing; huge amount of fear of shortcomings
- Possible challenges—holding feelings back for *so* long can finally result in a "breakdown" or some event happening because she cannot hold back any longer
- Possible addictions—can become addicted to having plastic surgery to accomplish their notion of perfection; no other addictions unless paired with other archetypes; if achievers do have an addiction, they will go to lengths to hide it (since that would mean they are not "perfect")

The Achiever—Defensive Behaviors

- Serenity mask
- Self-sufficiency and not needing help
- Works tirelessly for perfection—will work really hard to get every tiny detail perfect
- Can appear arrogant and aloof
- Fears and avoids vulnerability and determined to squash her true self as a result of that self being rejected in early childhood
- Other people may perceive behavior as cold, aloof, fake, superficial

The Achiever—Negative Thoughts/Statements/Core Beliefs

- Thoughts/statements—it is not safe to feel; I must be perfect; everything I do must be perfect; I am always fine; it is not safe to have, share, or express feelings; feelings are dangerous, messy, and out of my control, something to keep stifled and hidden; I can't surrender; I don't need anyone; life is a challenge, not a problem—chin up, chest out
- Possible negative core beliefs—if I am perfect, I am loved; if I am not perfect, I will be rejected and be without love; If I am perfect, I'll be allowed to live; if I

share my authentic self, I will lose love; I can't find my authentic self, it is too imperfect and too risky; intimacy will reveal my shortcomings, life needs to follow schedules, lists and patterns to be safe

- For female achievers—"If I want daddy to love me, I am not allowed to have any aliveness from the waist down (embody my sexuality)."

The Achiever—In Relationships

- Likes to be in a relationship or be married because it is what "you are supposed to do"
- Avoids real emotional connections when in a relationship
- Has to be in control of the relationship
- Does not like to "surrender" in any way
- Possible relationship challenges—when relationships start to crumble or achievers start to really "feel," they will have affairs as it is very hard for them to have sex with someone that they actually love and vice versa; achievers will minimize problems when in therapy

The Achiever—At Work/School

- Accomplished, ambitious, and driven—makes a good, fair leader with integrity
- Aims for perfection in everything she does

- Tries really hard to make straight As. A B would crush her (and disappoint her parents)
- Can easily become an athlete, CEO, or business owner
- Has very healthy boundaries and does not have problem saying "no" to others.
- Very organized and loves to plan (loves lists, project plans, etc.)—makes a good project manager
- Possible challenges—does not like to rearrange her schedule or change plans (once something is set, it is set); can be less than empathetic to someone on her team

The Achiever—Examples from Music, Film, TV, etc.

- Monica from *Friends*
- Jerry Seinfeld
- Steve Jobs
- Nicole Kidman
- Prince (+Dreamer)
- Annette Bening in *American Beauty*
- Hermione in *Harry Potter*
- Madonna (+Commander)

IN SUMMARY

How was that experience for you? Was it challenging, interesting, helpful, fun? Did it make you angry, sad, frustrated, curious? Maybe all of the above? And now, what do we do with *all* of this information? In the next chapter, we will look at all of your challenges and figure out what you want to work on.

Have a question about Come Alive? Send me your ideas, comments, questions and complaints. I want to know what you think. You can reach me at comealiveinstitute.com/contact.

CHAPTER 6

Step Three: Tackle Your Challenges

"Where you stumble and fall, there you will find gold."
–Joseph Campbell

I n this chapter you will look back at your dominant archetype(s) and identify your biggest challenges and figure out how to tackle them—that is, how to heal them or transform them to support you instead of hindering you. To help you do that, you are going to create your own inner supervillain!

I have also included many suggested tools and activities in this chapter, but these are only some of the possible ways of tackling these on your own.

IDENTIFYING YOUR BIGGEST CHALLENGES

When you look back at your archetypes, you will notice that there are positive traits, talents, and gifts on one side (the light) and negative traits, tendencies, and challenges (the shadow) on the other. Your shadows, or challenges, are really just defenses created to handle what you thought (as a child) was dangerous to you back then. Some of these defenses or challenges have helped you. They may have even saved your life in some respects.

So let's go back to the last chapter and identify your top five challenges in the three main areas (emotions/tendencies, behaviors, and beliefs). Look through your archetypes and see if you can identify challenges that are *really* bothering you right now and that you would like to tackle (change, heal, deal with). These can be challenges listed in the previous chapter or from your own self-knowledge. After you have identified them, document them in your journal—use the following as an example.

1. Top Five Negative Emotions and Tendencies

    • Anxiety/worry

    • Anger and frustration

- Fear of being seen/noticed
- Have a hard time asking for help
- Not being able to finish things
2. Top Five Defensive Behaviors
   - Scattered and unfocused
   - Procrastination
   - Not saying "no" when I want to
   - Taking on too much work
   - Not speaking my real truth (to my boss, partner)
3. Top Five Negative Thoughts/Beliefs
   - I can do it myself. I don't need any help.
   - Being truly seen can be dangerous.
   - I'll take care of it—whatever you want.
   - It is not safe to show my anger. I don't even know how to show it. I will just keep it inside.
   - I have to be in control to be safe.

TAKE ON THE CHALLENGES

Okay, now that you have documented your top challenges, it is time to tackle them! Throughout my work I have found the most common challenges, especially for women, are in the categories of: (1) Holding in: difficulty expressing or letting things out (emotions, thoughts); (2) Being Seen: fear of being seen or noticed; and (3) Boundaries: difficulty with setting boundaries and keeping them. There are many ways to tackle these challenges. I have included a few tools, activities, and self-care practices below organized by the most common categories of challenges. Look through these and try to identify which ones are applicable to you and see how they work. No need to do all of these.

INSIDE *OUT*

The tools in the section are good for getting what is going on inside you *out* of your head (or body). These are helpful for everyone, but they are especially helpful for challenges of both of the dreamer and endurer archetypes.

Activity—The Daily Muck and Shuck (Time Required: Ten to fifteen minutes)

Inspired by "Morning Pages" in Julia Cameron's *The Artist's Way*, I do a daily writing practice that I like to call the "Muck and Shuck." This is something that you can do first thing in the morning. I take ten to fifteen minutes and write freehand anything that comes to mind. This is a way of getting all of the "muck" inside your head *out* of your head and onto the page, where you can "shuck" it (forget it). For me, this includes any negative self-talk, my current worries, things that are making me frustrated or angry, or whatever is taking up space in my head that may interfere with me being present for the day. Do it for a couple of days and journal how it helped you (or didn't).

Activity—The Work Out (Time required: Twenty to thirty minutes with a partner, on phone)

The Work Out is an activity that you must do with another person, someone you trust (perhaps your partner on this journey). For the Work Out, you pick a topic that is causing you angst, something that you have been trying to "work out" in your head but are having a problem figuring out alone. The Work Out is specifically for you to get whatever is *in* your head about this topic *out* of your head so you can work it out. Doing a Work Out with someone else (if you both do one) should take about twenty to thirty minutes, so make sure you have the time and set boundaries around the time. The instructions are simple:

1. There are two roles: the talker and the witness. Decide who is going to go first (who the talker will be).
2. The talker chooses her topic (for example, "my job," "my marriage," "my relationship with money," "putting myself first," etc.).
3. Decide how much time to use (for example, five minutes). The witness sets her timer and asks the talker, "Are you ready to begin your Work Out on (chosen topic)?"

4. The witness then asks for a thought from the talker by saying, "What do you have on (chosen topic)?"

5. The talker says, "I have [whatever thought she has on the topic]" It should be one full statement and not a series of statements. No rambling or digressing allowed!

6. The witness only responds with "Thank you" to each thought (giving no additional feedback). Then she asks for another thought: "What do you have on [topic chosen]?"

7. This is repeated until the timer is up.

8. The witness then asks if the talker would like to say any additional thoughts (no more than three additional thoughts allowed).

9. Once done, the witness asks the talker if she would like to do a "Quad." A Quad includes a statement about the body, the emotions, and the mind and ends with a commitment to a self-care practice. A Quad goes like this: (1) "Right now I notice _____ in my body" (if she notices any sensations in her body), (2) "Right now I am feeling _____" (if she notices any emotions arising), (3) "Right now I am thinking _____" (if she notices any new thoughts or beliefs popping up), and (4) "I commit to my own self care by _____" (listing any desired self-care practices that come up). Example,

I commit to my own self-care by taking a long hot bath tonight to ensure I get a good night's sleep.

10. Once she is done, switch roles and repeat.

11. It is important to stay to the timing and the rules and for the witness to not give any feedback to the talker afterward unless she specifically asks for it *and* you have time. This allows the talker to process her Work Out in her own way and without judgment.

12. One extra note: after a Work Out, you may want to journal a bit as lots of ideas or creative thoughts may emerge after the experience.

This exercise is amazing at helping you work out an issue or problem. I have also found it very helpful to do a regular Work Out on a specific topic every day for a week or even a month.

Activity—Things Left Unsaid (Time required: Ten to fifteen minutes)

This activity is to get out the things that you never said to someone that you really wished you had said. These unsaid things tend to linger in our minds and bodies and can really hold you back from embodying your best self. This activity completely changed my client Danielle. She had no idea how much these unsaid things were holding her back in her life until she started doing this activity on regular basis. It really brought her out of her shell. Once she wrote these things down and said them out loud to me, they lost their power over her. She even got enough courage to actually tell a few people these unsaid things. It completely changed her relationships, and she had so much more confidence.

Try it yourself—start writing in your journal things you left unsaid. For example, "I never told Tom that I loved him," "I never told my sister how much it hurt when she gave away mom's things," or "I never told my boss that I really deserved a raise." Write for as long as you can (usually lasts no more than fifteen minutes).

Extra bonus: after you are done, find a trusted partner and read them aloud. This exercise is very powerful once you read it aloud.

Activity—Fear Inventory (Time required: Ten minutes)

This is an activity to document all the fears going on inside your head. Write this on sheets of paper that you can throw away (not in your journal). This is a *great* activity to do every morning.

The instructions are very simple.

1. Complete the following: "God [or Universe or Higher Power], I am resentful that I _____ because I have fear that I _____."

2. Keep going until you run out of steam (five to ten minutes). Write as many of the fears that are in your head as you can.

3. Once you are done, write the following: "God, I ask that you remove these fears. I pray only for knowledge of your will for us and the power to carry that out for me, and [my family, friends, colleagues, and loved ones. Feel free to name individuals here.]"

4. Then take the papers you have written on and tear them up and throw them away (or burn them).

BEING SEEN/NOTICED/ATTENTION

The tools in the section are good for tackling the fear of being seen, heard, or noticed. Again, these are helpful for everyone, but they are especially helpful for challenges of the dreamer, charmer, and endurer archetypes.

Activity—Mirror Work (Time required: Five minutes or less)

1. Go into your bathroom and look in the mirror.

2. Really gaze into your own eyes. Rest there for a few seconds.

3. Now say "I love me" slowly over and over while gazing into your own eyes. Do this for as long as you can—at least a minute or two.

4. What comes up for you? Tears are normal.

5. Now raise your hands up, as if you are a little girl wanting your mom to come pick you up and say "I need" slowly over and over. Do this for at least a minute or two.

6. What comes up for you? Tears are normal.

7. Give yourself a gratitude! This exercise is harder than it sounds.

Activity—Noticing (Time required: Ten to fifteen minutes with a partner, in person)

1. Get a partner and sit somewhere where you can face each other directly.

2. First gaze into each other's eyes for two minutes (time it) with no words or sounds.

3. What comes up for you? Did it make you uncomfortable?

4. Now take turns being the noticer.

5. The noticer looks at her partner and starts noticing things about her and says things like, "You have two eyes, you have two ears. You have a big smile. You are wearing a blue shirt with buttons on it." Whatever they notice about the other person.

6. The noticer will continue for two minutes, trying not to break eye contact.

7. After the timer goes off, the noticer finishes with "You are enough" slowly three times while gazing into their eyes and smiling.

8. Discuss your experience. What comes up for both of you?

9. Switch roles and repeat.

10. Again discuss your experience. What comes up for both of you?

SETTING BOUNDARIES

The tools in the section are good for tackling the difficulty in setting boundaries, which is helpful to the dreamer and endurer archetypes.

Tool—Boundaries Excuse List

Setting boundaries is especially hard for the endurer archetype. I had a client, Janine, who was working two jobs and was completely exhausted. She was really an artist but had no time or energy to pursue it. She took on way too much at both jobs and never seemed to "get a break" as she said. We worked together on setting boundaries, but she said it was so hard to do in the moment when someone asks her to do something. She hated disappointing others and was not "quick on her feet." We came up with a boundary excuse list that she could use as a kind of cheat sheet when someone would ask her to do something that she did want to do, did not have time or energy to do, or was not in her best interest to do. Below is a sampling from her list:

- No, I am sorry I cannot. (This one was really hard for her!)
- I am working on setting boundaries, and this is not something that would be in my best interest to do right now. But I appreciate you asking me.
- (for work) I am not the best fit for this task as my plate is already full. Why don't you ask _____ to help you out?
- (for work) I am not the best qualified person for this. I would ask ____ to help you out.
- I would love to, but I am only going to events that really jazz me and this does not really do that. Thank you for asking and have fun!
- That sounds like fun, but I planned to paint tonight and I am going to stick to my plan. I hope you enjoy yourself.
- (for a date that she did not want to go on) I like you, but I don't see us being a match and I do not want to

waste your time or my time. But thank you for asking. I wish you the best.

Now create your own list and have it handy so you can use it. Keep in mind the excuse has to be true to use it! This is a really fun list to create.

Tool—Setting Containers

A container is a set of expectations or rules that you set up for things like a relationship, an event, a meeting, or even a conversation. Setting a container is very important in certain situations. For example, a client, Maria, was having drinks with a coworker to talk about work when all of a sudden, he said something that offended her and it was hard for her to get back on track and made it very awkward for them both. She clammed up and felt like she was being taken advantage of. Setting a container for something like this would have been very powerful. We agreed that in the future, she could set a container that might look like this: "John, I would like to set up a container for this meeting. We are here to talk about work, and I would like to stick to work topics. I have thirty minutes. Does that work for you?"

Explore setting containers for conversations to start with and see how it works. I find it works really well for conversations with people who tend to talk too much. Then you can move on to meetings, events, and even relationships.

Okay, did any of the above tools or activities resonate with you? These are just a few of the activities from the Come Alive program. Practicing the activities that resonate with you on a regular basis can make a huge difference in your life. If you decide to practice some, please make notes in your journal about which ones really made a difference and how.

Now that you have identified your top challenges and played with a few of the tools and activities, let's move on to the pinnacle of tackling your challenges—creating your own supervillain! This is getting exciting!

A LITTLE BIT ABOUT HEROES AND VILLAINS

Remember that your challenges are really just defenses created to handle what you thought (as a child) was dangerous to you back then.

What if we take your top challenges from what you identified earlier and "assign" them to your own *supervillain* who is living inside you? And what if we take all of the light side of your archetypes and assign that to your own *superhero* living inside you? And what if that could help repair the damage of those challenges by doing that?

I have done this myself and with my clients, and it is so surprising how powerful, healing, and fun it is! If you are more comfortable using "your light" and "your shadow" (or "your dark") instead of "superhero" or "supervillain," feel free. I prefer superhero and supervillain, but I am a nerd!

YOUR INNER SUPERVILLAIN

Supervillains are not really bad, just misunderstood. If you think of most supervillains in comic books or movies, they were damaged souls whose defenses or challenges got the better of them.

So let's start to create your own supervillain! Once you have your supervillain created, you can talk to it—ask it questions, ask it what it wants and why it is here. This is not only fun, but very informative. I know it may sound childish or a little weird, but you will be surprised at the answers it will give you!

With that said, let's look back at what you identified earlier and complete the supervillain worksheet!

SUPERVILLAIN WORKSHEET

The supervillain worksheet is a fun way to compile all of your top challenges along with strategies on how to tackle them. Complete the items below in your journal or download a copy of worksheet in the toolkit here: http://comealiveinstitute.com/toolkit.

- **Name**: Give your supervillain a name. You may want to do this after you have filled in more of the sheet.

- **Sex**: Is it male or female? Or maybe unisex or gender neutral?

- **Physical Traits**: What are some of the physical traits you want your supervillain to have? Think of physical traits that you don't like about yourself. Or some physical traits from one of your dominant archetypes.

- **Traits**: What are some of the negative traits you want to assign to your supervillain? Go back and look to see what you highlighted in Chapter 5. These should be traits that you do not like about yourself. Or maybe even traits that you really don't like about others.

- **Your supervillain special powers/your defenses:** What are some of your biggest challenges that you identified earlier? These include the tendencies, emotions, and behaviors. Think of ones that are particularly challenging or that you really wish you did *not* have. Those are good ones! Be as outrageous, nasty, and fun as you wish. This is your chance to be really bad!

- **"Weapons of choice"/sabotaging beliefs**: Document any core beliefs that you identified earlier in this chapter. Add those beliefs here. Continue to add to this as you discover more beliefs.

MAKING IT REAL

Now that you have documented your supervillain, you may want to make it more real. If you draw or know someone who draws, try to get a picture of it. Or you can try an online generator like heromachine.com to create your own supervillain. If you can, try to get or print a physical copy of it so that it is a real display of your supervillain. You can also create a sock puppet of it or even use an action figure. It is important to have something physical to interact with.

Keep your physical supervillain handy, as we will use it in an activity in the next chapter, alongside your superhero! And don't forget to post your supervillain on the Come Alive Facebook Group.

IN SUMMARY

How was this chapter for you? Was it hard, frustrating, too much information? Was it intriguing, eye-opening, or maybe even exciting? Do you feel different? I am hoping that you feel much lighter than you did before. Moving forward is going to be so much easier now.

Remember to take your time with this chapter and this part of the process. This is the hard stuff, and it is important to get it right.

Now that we have identified and tackled some of your challenges, let's move on to your gifts and talents—to restoring your brilliance!

CHAPTER 7

Step Four: Restore Your Brilliance

> *"All the gods, all the heavens,*
> *all the hells, are within you."*
> –Joseph Campbell

I n this chapter you will look back at your dominant archetypes and identify your greatest gifts and talents and discover how to nurture them to fully support you. I have
included many suggested self-care practices and activities in this
chapter, but these are only a few of the many possible ways of
supporting yourself on your own.

YOUR INNER SUPERHERO

It is now time to create your own inner superhero focusing on your gifts and talents but also adding strategies to battle your inner supervillain. So let's go back to Chapter 5 and identify your top five to ten gifts and talents—that is, the talents that you currently use and are most proud of, as well as the ones you know are inside you but maybe have not had a chance to use lately or have not cultivated yet.

And then let's identify what "weapons of choice" you will use to fend off your supervillain. That is, what self-care practices will you arm yourself with to strengthen your superhero?

To make it easy, I have included a snapshot of each archetype below. The snapshots include a summary of the archetype plus suggested self-care practices.

THE DREAMER—SNAPSHOT

- **True essence**—creativity
- **Biggest gifts**—brilliance, innovation, visionary, independent, artistic, intuitive, problem-solver
- **Needs to learn**—to feel safe in her body, to know that it is safe to connect with others, to get out of her head
- **Suggested self-care practices**—doing a fear inventory every day; grounding meditation or three-body check-in; deep breathing; moving body; dancing; con-

nection with another human being (talking or in-person contact); hugging someone (ask for hugs!); allowing yourself to scream (primal scream) in a safe space; making a plan of action—walking through the fear; sensorial things—taking a warm bath, massage, touch, aromatherapy, being with and touching animals, spending time in nature, using a weighted blanket, anything that makes you feel like you are part of this earth and belong here; having a "support buddy" that you can call or be in person with; setting safe *containers* and boundaries for your interactions with others; making your physical environment safe and comfortable (design, colors, lighting furniture, clutter)

THE CHARMER—SNAPSHOT

- **True essence**—love
- **Biggest gifts**—charm, persuasiveness, speaking, writing, performing, collaboration
- **Needs to learn**—to own her needs and find own power, to be able to stand on her own two feet (with no help from anyone else), to experience and acknowledge fullness so she can re-create it on her own, to learn how to dominate/lead someone else, to truly give with no expectation of getting something in return

- **Suggested self-care practices**—asking yourself, "What do I need?"; grounding; breathing; hot baths; sunbathing; walking; feeding the senses—music, art; being in nature; integrating with words; setting boundaries; massage; bodywork; swimming—breast stroke; dance class; yoga

THE ENDURER—SNAPSHOT

- **True essence**—compassion
- **Biggest gifts**—empathetic, intuitive, sensitive, thoughtful, helpful, productive
- **Needs to learn**—to get what is inside *out*, to know that it is safe to fully express emotions, to fully express what is inside (her truth), to take criticism without falling apart, to set boundaries and not take on anyone else's "stuff"
- **Suggested self-care practices**—doing a fear inventory every day; experimenting with telling people "no"; dis-identifying with the inner critic—asking "who is saying that?" in your head (your father, mother, sister); practicing forgiveness with family members; anger therapy (beating your bed and screaming in a safe space); scheduling time to emote—to cry, to get angry—and getting used to letting emotions *out* of the body in a safe manner and space

THE COMMANDER—SNAPSHOT

- **True essence**—devotion, leadership
- **Biggest gifts**—leadership, vision, loyalty, courage, charisma, risk-taker
- **Needs to learn**—how to apologize; to be OK with being "wrong"; to let others lead; to gain trust and allow herself to be vulnerable to others; to balance power with heart; to feel a state of surrender without defeat
- **Suggested self-care practices**—practice letting someone else lead or take the reins from you (on a project or at home); practice apologizing to someone (even *if* you do not believe you need to); practice admitting you are wrong to someone (even *if* you do believe you are right); cry; scream; throw temper tantrums; grieve over lost childhood; write a letter (that you do not send) to your parents; make a plan; work out at the gym; dance; speed-walk in nature

THE ACHIEVER—SNAPSHOT

- **True essence**—integrity
- **Biggest gifts**—fairness, balance, quality, beauty, organization, boundaries

- **Needs to learn**—to surrender to imperfection, that it is safe to get in touch with and show emotions, that it is OK to not be the best at everything
- **Suggested self-care practices**—doing the three-body check-in every day; getting massages; sharing your feelings with your partner, friends, and family; asking others to reflect your emotions back to you; practicing leaving your home or desk cluttered and seeing what that brings up for you; letting someone else win and seeing how that feels; practicing being vulnerable with a friend or partner

SUPERHERO WORKSHEET

Now complete the superhero worksheet below in your journal or download the worksheet in the toolkit here:

http://comealiveinstitute.com/toolkit.

- **Name**: Give your superhero a name. You may want to do this after you have filled in more of the sheet.
- **Sex**: Is it male or female? Or maybe unisex?
- **Physical Traits**: What are some of the physical traits you want your supervillain to have?
- **Traits**: What are some of the positive traits you want to assign to your superhero? Go back and look to see what you highlighted in the last chapter. Add some spice and some fun.

- **Your superhero special powers/your gifts:** What are some of your greatest gifts that you identified earlier? Think of ones that you really want to use and cultivate. Again, be as outrageous as you wish. This is your chance to be really fun and cool!
- **"Weapons of choice"/strategies for tackling your supervillain defenses**: Look back at the specific self-care practices that helped with tackling your challenges and defenses. These are the "weapons" your superhero will use to fight off your supervillain.

MAKING IT REAL

As with your supervillain, you will want to create a physical copy of your superhero. Either a drawing, a printout of an online-generated one, a decorated sock puppet, or an action figure. It is important to have something physical to interact with. And don't forget to post your superhero on the Come Alive Facebook Group.

Once you have it created, you now have both your supervillain and superhero! And guess what? They can now have a conversation!

WE NEED TO TALK

Now let's do an activity with both your supervillain and superhero. It is important to do this activity with another person (as a witness).

Activity—The Super Talk (Required Time: Twenty to thirty minutes for two people, with a partner, in person)

Taking turns with a partner, have your superhero and super-villain ready to have a conversation. Once ready, each of you will take turns and act out the following:

1. Superhero will ask supervillain the following questions. The supervillain will respond with whatever immediately comes up. Don't think too hard, just say what comes to mind first.

    •   What do you want?
    •   Why?
    •   Why do you (always) do [name a defense, patter or belief]?
    •   What will make you feel safe?
    •   What will make you feel satisfied?
    •   How can I help?

2. Then flip it and have the supervillain ask the superhero the same questions.

3. Discuss the experience with your partner.

4. Then take turns and repeat.

Now you can have a conversation between the two of them whenever you want and *know* that they are both there to support you in living the life you came to live! This is an incredible exercise to do on a regular basis, whenever you are stuck in any situation. It is most beneficial with a partner to witness, but you can do this alone.

Adjust both your supervillain and superhero worksheets as necessary to always be up-to-date with where you are. And remember that tacking and healing your challenges is a process and takes time but having all of these tools and practices to choose from really helps give you a jumpstart. Many of us still need to go see professionals such as psychotherapists, mind-body practitioners, and body workers to continue our journey to wholeness and aliveness.

IN SUMMARY

How was this chapter for you? Was it fun, interesting? Do you feel different? Try to journal every day for a week after this to see what has changed for you. Do you feel more like yourself? Are you calmer and more confident than before? Are desires starting to rise? Is your passion starting to flame? That means it is time to move on to Chapter 8, "Step Five: Honing Your Desires"!

CHAPTER 8

Step Five: Hone Your Desires

"We're so engaged in doing things to achieve purposes of outer value that we forget the inner value, the rapture that is associated with being alive, is what it is all about."
–Joseph Campbell

I n this chapter we will shift the focus to passion and desire. Now that you have assessed yourself, explored your archetypes, identified and started to tackle your biggest challenges, and identified and accepted your true talents and gifts, with the help of your supervillain and superhero, you are now ready to truly tune into your real desires, your passions.

THE IMPORTANCE OF DESIRE

A couple of years ago when I took Foundations of Power with Kasia Urbaniak, I learned that desire is something that resides within each of us, always. And it is something that you do not have control over. You desire what you desire. But it is hard to tune into it with all of the other things that get in the way—your past trauma, what your family, partner, or friends want you to do, what you went to school for, what kind of job you think you can make money doing, etc. But *none* of those things have anything to do with desire. Desire is a longing inside of you. It is a magnet for your own true north, your purpose, your passion. And when you truly tune into it, your whole world changes.

Many of us are not used to thinking about our real desires because we have always been taking care of others—our children, our partners, our aging parents, etc. Our needs and desires have always been put on the back burner. But the truth is when we, especially as women, put our desires on hold, the whole world suffers. When you are in tune with your desires, you come *alive,* and when you are fully alive, you have a ripple effect on everyone around you. It can, quite literally, change the world!

Most people, especially women, don't know the first thing about tuning into our desires. And we need practice. So let's start small, with little desires. Right now, speak or write down ten desires quickly. Whatever comes to mind. Here are a few of mine: I want ice cream (like right now), I want to get a good night's sleep tonight, I desire to take a long hot bath with yummy essential oils, I want to take a salsa dancing lesson, I desire to go to Croatia this summer and swim in the Adriatic.

CULTIVATE A DESIRE PRACTICE

To get used to expressing your desires, find a partner to help you cultivate a desire practice. Call that person every day (if you can) and speak five to ten desires. Start writing a "desire inventory" in your journal every morning (it's very beneficial if you do it right after your fear inventory). Try to write for five to ten minutes straight, as many desires as you can think of. Desires big and small. Get used to "living in desire." Your world will start to change. You will see things and people differently.

Look back at what you wrote down in Chapter 4 about what brings you joy or pleasure (as a child and now). Do those still resonate with you? Are there hidden desires there? Look at them and see if you can rewrite some of those in "I desire …" form.

THE SUPER CHECK-IN

Once you get some desire practice under your belt, it is time to check in with your superhero and supervillain again. If you have already been practicing talking to or checking in with both your supervillain and superhero, this will be pretty easy for you. You can do this alone or with a partner, whatever works for you.

First ask your supervillain: What do you truly desire? What is behind that desire? Do not judge the answer. Write it down in your journal. Then shift over to your superhero and ask the same two questions, again with no judgment, and write it down. Look at those desires. How do they feel to you? Let those desires marinate with you for a day or two or even a week.

THE *BIG* DESIRES

Okay, now it's time to get to the *big* desires. What do I mean by that? I am talking about the things that are *really* important to you, desires that are related to your passion and your purpose. Because at this point, they should begin to bubble up inside you. And some of them may surprise you. Think about what is going to make you truly happy and fulfilled. Is it a new career? Is it starting your own business? Is it getting promoted? Is it making a million dollars? Is it adding hobbies or the arts back into your life? Is it a new relationship? Is it repairing a relationship? Is it living in a different city or country? Is it moving to a new house?

Go back and look at your Self-Care Wheel and see if a new desire pops up for you.

When you feel a very clear big desire bubbling up, write it down. Sit with it. Once you are comfortable with it, then do the Three-Body Desire Check-In to validate that it is true for you.

Activity—The Three-Body Desire Check-In (time required—ten to fifteen minutes)

1. Sit comfortably in a chair with your back straight, feet on the floor, and your journal close by.
2. Write a big desire in your journal in the form of *I desire …*
3. Then close your eyes, regulate your breathing, and have that desire clear in your mind.
4. Then check-in with your *physical body*. Write down any sensations or feelings in your body about this desire. Once done, thank your physical body for serving you today.
5. Move on to the *emotional body*. Again notice your breath, regulate it, and again have the desire clear in your mind. With eyes closed, ask yourself how you are feeling emotionally about this desire? Does it excite you? Write down whatever emotions come up for you around this desire. Again, thank your emotions for serving you today.

6. Move on to the mind, the *mental body*. Once more, notice your breath and regulate it as best you can. Ask yourself what thoughts or beliefs are popping up about this desire. Write them down. Once done, thank your beliefs for serving you today.

7. Repeat this process three times. Yes, three times. You will be amazed at what comes up when you have a legitimate, true desire that truly resonates with your whole being.

8. End with an overall gratitude to all three bodies and for your desires.

This exercise should really solidify a *big* desire for you. If the desire changed during this exercise, modify it in your journal. Do this exercise with every big desire that comes bubbling up for you, no matter how outrageous it may seem for you. It could be something like "I desire to buy a farm in France and host retreats there." Nothing is impossible when you truly connect to desire.

YOUR PASSION STATEMENT

Once you have enough practice tuning into your big desires, you are ready to write what I call your "passion statement." This statement is really more of a paragraph. It will encompass all of your big desires. And it is written in the present tense, even though they have not come true yet.

Here is my passion statement that I mentioned earlier in the book:

I am a wealthy, wildly successful, celebrated author, coach, educator, speaker, and entrepreneur. I am the author of the Come Alive book series and creator of the Come Alive program and retreats. I live and work in a beautiful place near water and a forest, preferably in Europe. And I have a wonderful man in my life.

BROADCAST YOUR SIGNAL

Once you get *super* clear and specific on your desires and write your passion statement, post it on your wall. Meditate on it. Every day. Start telling people about it. Have it in your mind all the time. This is how you broadcast your signal to the world. When you do this, it ignites your passion and amazing things start to happen.

I worked with a client, Randa, who was completely miserable working in the corporate world. She liked what she did but hated working for a big corporation and hated where she lived. She was super smart, creative, and artistic, but all of her uniqueness and creativity were being squashed working for small-minded bosses. Her corporate job paid the bills, but she wanted to be creative, to be able do her photography. Her biggest pain points were working for someone else and where she lived. She got super clear and specific in her desires and validated them.

She really wanted to work for herself and live in the Netherlands. She had no idea how it was going to happen, but she started broadcasting her signal. Within six months, she was living in the Hague, running her own consulting firm, and doing her photography on top. And she gets to go to the beach every day. And she is a completely different person. And so is everyone around her.

When I wrote my passion statement, things started to happen *very* quickly for me. Like within a week. It was a bit unnerving how powerful this practice truly is. All the answers to everything are inside you! And you are powerful beyond measure. You can make things happen just by broadcasting the *right* signal to the Universe. The right signal being your true passion and purpose. And keep on the lookout how others around you change as a result: your family, your friends, colleagues, people on the street, etc. You finding and living your true passion has a positive ripple effect in the world.

IN SUMMARY

How are you feeling now? I hope you are feeling like you are on fire! Alive and aflame with your desires powering you. Let's move onto the last step, Manifestation!

CHAPTER 9

Step Six: Manifest Your True Passion

*"Follow your bliss and the universe will open doors
for you where there were only walls."*
–Joseph Campbell

I n this chapter, we will cover the last step in the process, Manifesting Your True Passion. We have cultivated all the seeds; now it is time to make it all happen and prepare yourself for success.

BUILD YOUR SUCCESS PROFILE

Now that you have gotten crystal clear on your passion statement and have started broadcasting your signal, it is time to build what I call your "success profile." Things will start happening for you quickly, and you need to be ready for them.

What is in a success profile? Your success profile helps you envision and craft your outcome. It incorporates four things and can be put in a Word doc or on a poster board (like a vision board) or can be posted online (as long you see it *every* day). Divide the page or poster into four quadrants and include the following four things:

1. Your passion statement: you may have honed it a bit so put the most recent version of it.

2. Your success measures: come up with three to five things that would prove or validate that your passion statement has come true or is successful. Think *big*! For my statement, it included things like:

   • My book series is a best seller on Amazon and the New York Times. It has sold over a million copies.

   • I get invited to be on Oprah's Super Soul Sunday.

   • I have a Ted Talk published online that has more than a million views.

   • My programs and retreats are sold out and have a waiting list.

- I live or work in France, Italy, or Switzerland.

3. Success scene: Write a "scene" like in a movie that describes an event in the future where your success has already happened. Be very specific and write it in the present tense. Publish it in the Facebook Group.

4. Visual images of your success: Find and post pictures that embody your new success. They can include anything from your success measures or your scene.

Look at your success profile every day. Speak it out loud. Meditate on it. Think about it often. Update it as you see fit.

PICK YOUR THEME SONG

Okay, now it is time to pick a "theme song." Yes, that's right. Your own theme song. Picking a theme song is so much fun! Some of you will know immediately what song to pick. And you can always change it. My first one was "Say the Word" by my favorite local band at the time, Ten Hands. I had that one for a decade. My next one was "Golden" by Jill Scott for about seven years. Now it's, you guessed it, "Come Alive" from the Greatest Showman soundtrack. If you have not seen that film, put this book down right now and go watch it. It's magical and wonderful! And get the soundtrack. Some other favorites on that soundtrack include "This Is Me," which is another great theme song.

The only requirement for your theme song is that it MUST make you come *alive* when you hear it. Your eyes light up and you want to dance, clean the kitchen, rule the world, whatever. Once you've picked it, try to listen to that song every day if you can. Music has a way of taking us out of our heads and into our bodies and helps tremendously with manifestation. Listen to it while looking at your success profile.

CREATE OR UPDATE YOUR PERSONAL BRAND

This is where the rubber meets the road. You need to be ready for your new success. Do you have/need a personal brand? By that, I mean the following:

- Personal look and style (hair, clothes, makeup, etc.)
- Social media presence (LinkedIn, Instagram, Facebook, Twitter)
- Business cards or other collateral
- Personal or business website
- New photos of yourself
- Up-to-date résumé

If your passion and outcome include business success, then you need to be ready for it. Updating your style can make all the difference in the world. Hiring an expert in personal branding may be necessary. You also may want to update your wardrobe or your home to fit your new style. Look for resources on our website.

You may even want to plan a launch party for yourself. Like a debut of the new you, alive with passion and desire! Invite all your friends and family and have fun. Post pictures on the Facebook Group.

UPSKILL WHERE NEEDED

Does your new passion include learning new skills? If so, check out sites like Udemy or LinkedIn Learning and build a curriculum so that you can get up to speed as quick as you can. Start following people in your industry on LinkedIn, Twitter, or Instagram. Subscribe to news sources that will help you with your new passion or even start your own blog.

If your passion includes starting your own business or updating your current business, you may want to look into taking some business classes, such as Marie Forleo's B-School. If your passion includes publishing a book that makes a difference, consider the Author Incubator like I did. Look for additional resources on our website.

HABITS TO CULTIVATE

As things start to happen for you, make sure you continue with some of the regular practices that you learned here as well as cultivating new habits so that you are always moving forward. Some good habits to cultivate include:

1. Meditate or do the Three-Body Check-in every day (or at least once a week)

2. Do a fear inventory once a week.

3. Do a desire inventory once a week.

4. Keep your supervillain and superhero nearby for frequent conversation practice and check-ins. They will keep you on track.

5. Make note of any big desires coming up from the previous two points. If so, do a Three-Body Desire Check-in to validate.

6. Look at your passion statement and success profile every day. Update as you see fit. Meditate on it as much as you can.

7. Keep sharing on the Facebook Group for your own success as well as helping others with their success

SELF-CARE WHEEL CHECK-IN

Remember the Self-Care Wheel activity we did in the beginning? Let's take that out again and look at it. Update it to where you are now. Did you take a new photo of yourself and compare it to the first one? How have you changed? Did you improve? Please post your success stories to the Facebook Group:

https://www.facebook.com/groups/comealivebook

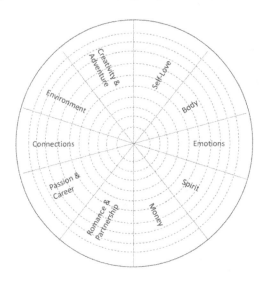

IN SUMMARY

We have come to the end of the Come Alive process. How do you feel? Are you a changed person? Are you more in touch with yourself, your challenges, your talents, and your desires? Are you interested in learning what is next? If so, move forward.

CHAPTER 10

You Made It This Far!

> *"If the path before you is clear,*
> *you're probably on someone else's."*
> –Joseph Campbell

THIS IS HARD WORK

No doubt the Come Alive process is hard. Looking at yourself and facing your challenges and tackling them does not come easy. Congratulations for making it this far! Most of us spend our whole lives ignoring them or running away from them and just doing the "safe thing." But how is that working out? Not so good, right? Remember in the movie *Alien* toward the end when Ripley (Sigourney Weaver) tries to escape the alien creature by sneaking away on the shuttle? But as soon as she got "comfortable" thinking she was safe, there it was—the creature, on the shuttle with her. She could not get rid of it until she battled it face to face. That is the same with your challenges, issues, demons, or whatever you want to call them. Coming face to face with them (acknowledging them) and then tackling them is the only way to get rid of them or disempower them from holding you back in life. It is the only way to make a clear path for your passion to rise up to become the person you were meant to be. To become fully alive!

GUIDANCE IS KEY

Because this process is so hard, not everyone completes it or sticks with it. At least not without help or guidance. I certainly did not. But the right guidance is key. I was in traditional talk therapy for well over a decade and it was *not* helping me anymore. It was not until I went to Lionheart and started working with mind-body practitioners that I truly transformed my challenges, my demons, into something that supported me instead of hindered me. It was not an overnight process. It took some time, but the results were immediate and powerful.

That is why I designed the Come Alive program to go with the book. Everyone's journey is unique, and you are not meant to go through this alone. So many of the practices and activities in the process are meant to be done in the presence of another person, a guide.

MARY'S STORY

When I first met Mary, I thought she had it all together. She was beautiful and fit, the mother of three amazing adult children, and independently wealthy. What more could one want, right? But inside Mary was a mess—a ball of anxiety, so afraid to do the "wrong" thing at every turn. But the thing that caused her the greatest anxiety—"I don't know what my passion is. I don't want to live the rest of my life without knowing and living it."

Mary grew up very wealthy and never had to work, so it wasn't so much that she needed a career to make money. But she needed fulfillment, to live a life of purpose. I remember having a conversation with her where she said "Jodi, you are so much better off than me."

I said back to her, "How do you figure that? You have over a million dollars in your bank account!"

She said, "You know your passion, and you are doing it. I would give anything for that." Mary was a creative soul with so many talents, but because she never "had to work," she never really did much with them. She was living in fear and shame that she was wealthy and unhappy. She was afraid to ask for help, to admit she was not "perfect."

Mary's dominant archetypes were dreamer, commander, and achiever. After working with Mary for over a year, tackling her fears and challenges, she is now making gorgeous jewelry, playing the guitar and singing (actually playing gigs!), and traveling the world to look at art. On top of that, she has found an amazing man that she is crazy about. These were all her true inner desires; some of them she was not even aware of until she did the work of identifying and tackling her challenges. She is now living her passion! And she is OK with being "wrong" about things and not having to do everything perfectly. Does she still have fears and anxiety? Sure. But in tiny amounts. And she has many tools to use to fight off her supervillain whenever she wants.

CHAPTER 11

Your Journey Is Unique

"As you go the way of life, you will see a great chasm.
Jump. It is not as wide as you think."
–Joseph Campbell

THE END OF THE COME ALIVE

We have reached the end of our journey together. At least book-wise, we have. This is the part that makes me sad. I want to stay connected with all of my readers and program participants.

Let's recap the process. We started with an assessment of where you were (self-care wheel), what your interests were, and what your dominant archetypes are. Then we moved onto exploring your archetypes and identifying your challenges and gifts. Next, we moved on to facing and tackling your biggest challenges (the *big* step) and creating your own supervillain to support you in this step. Then we moved on to identifying your greatest talents and gifts, creating your own superhero and coming up with strategies to keep your supervillain at bay and restore your brilliance. Then we were ready to head into the land of desire, tuning into and honing your true desires (with the help of your supervillain and superhero) and creating your passion statement. Then finally moving into manifestation with creating your success profile, creating or updating your brand, and upskilling where needed. And *bam*, you are ready for lift off: passion ignited!

THE COME ALIVE CREED

At Come Alive, we believe your success on this journey is based on the following ten beliefs:

1. We are all put on this earth with a real purpose. And that purpose affects the world, for good.
2. That purpose comprises our true passion and our true desires residing within us. Those desires have always there, but perhaps just not ignited or realized yet.

3. We are all human and, therefore, have experienced trauma, starting from the moment we were conceived.

4. The result of this trauma comes in the form of our developmental archetypes.

5. These archetypes include both positive and negative patterns and tendencies that direct our personal and professional lives.

6. The negative patterns and tendencies have caused damage that is likely masking the path to our true passion and desires. This damage comes in the form of our challenges in life.

7. To uncover our real passion and desires, we must identify those challenges and be willing to face them and tackle them, to repair them.

8. We are all capable of making repairs, of making real change, of healing ourselves. And sometimes we need guidance along the way.

9. Once we decide to make these repairs, all our true talents and "superpowers" can fully emerge. We are able to connect to our true desires, our true passion, and our real purpose with ease.

10. There is no "one size fits all" solution for this. Each person creates their unique solution, designed to tackle their personal challenges, to realize and own their own

unique talents, and to connect to and manifest their true desires.

MY WISH FOR YOU

Your journey to your true purpose and passion is yours and yours alone. Try not to compare your journey or your passion or your desires to anyone else. And don't let the Joneses get you down!

My wish for you is to *not* live in fear. To *go for* things that you truly desire regardless of what others think. To not hide. To speak up for yourself and stand up for your passion. To truly tune in to your true desires and live the life you came to live. To not waste another minute or another dollar going down the wrong path or living a life that does not matter. The choice is yours. You just have to step into it.

NEXT STEPS

By now, you should know your passion and have a clear path to making it happen. If you are not, do not despair! It is easy to get stuck and need some more guidance. Move forward to the thank-you page for information on how to get help.

Further Reading

The 5 Personality Patterns by Steven Kessler
The Undefended Self by Susan Thesenga
Healing Developmental Trauma by Laurence Heller and Aline LaPierre
The Language of the Body by Alexander Lowen
Hands of Light by Barbara Ann Brennan
Light Emerging by Barbara Ann Brennan
Character Analysis by Wilhelm Reich

Acknowledgments

There are so many people who helped make this book happen. I first want to thank two of my closest friends, Melani Meyer and Donna Synodis, who have believed in me and supported me every step of the way in this amazing journey. I could not have done this without you. I want to thank Marty Avary for being my true sister through both Lionheart and Mama Gena's and so much more. I want to thank my dear friend Cynthia Savelli, who has always supported me no matter what. I want to thank all of my Lionheart teachers, who were so brilliant and fierce in their teachings, coaching, and healing—Dan Buffo, Laura Fine, Deb Allen, Scott Bader, Sandra Pribanic, Nino Seko-pet, and Sheryl Grant. I especially want to call out Dan Buffo for helping me heal my adrenal exhaustion so quickly and Deb Allen for her undying support and her amazing women's circles she holds around the world. I want to thank my amazing life coach, Lisa Carmen, for giving me the tools I needed so badly and supporting me in such a loving and passionate way. I want to thank Mama Gena for creating such an amazing community of sisterhood. I want to thank all of my close "sister goddesses" who supported me through this journey, most especially Valerie Bennis, Mikelle Terson, Amy Bliss, Terri-Marie Asous, Jennifer Benetato, Andrea Talbot, Jane Aptaker, Caitlin Stilin-Rooney, Deb Polo and Heather Symone. I want to thank Kadena Tate Simon for being my first business coach and for introducing me to Kasia Urbaniak. I want to thank Kasia Urbaniak and her partner, Ruben Flores, for creating and executing an amazing curriculum on female empowerment, and I want to thank all the mistresses in my cohort (you know who you are). I want to thank Rudy McCallum for being there to support me and for being my guinea pig on so much of the content for the book. I want to thank my personal trainer Chris Weigel for constantly reminding me to live a life of passion while I was his client (it finally sunk in!). I want to thank Mark D'Aquin for always supporting my creative ideas and helping me with any of my design needs. I want to thank Christine Gauthreaux for her undying support of my book, program and business. Thank you to David

Hancock and the Morgan James Publishing team for helping me bring this book to print. I want to thank my amazing editor, Bethany Davis, who was so supportive and inspirational in her edits. And last but certainly not least, I want to thank Angela Lauria—without you this book would not have been published. I am so glad I found out about you and that I took a chance to submit my idea and that you accepted me and supported me so fully. It's been a blast!

Thank You

hank you for reading my book! I would love to hear more about your experience and your journey to passion. Please email me at info@comealiveinstitute.com.

SHARE YOUR SUCCESS

If you go through the Come Alive process (either through the book or program), I invite you to share your success on our Facebook group (https://www.facebook.com/groups/comealive-book). Sharing your success can help you as well as others who are in the process.

NEED GUIDANCE AND READY TO "GO FOR IT"?

Are you interested in exploring deeper? I invite you to investigate if the Come Alive program is for you. How to know if you are a candidate for the Come Alive program:

- You know you were born to live your passion
- You are ready to face and tackle your biggest fears and challenges head on
- You are ready to accept your true gifts and talents and actually use them
- You want to connect to your desires
- You want to make a difference in the world
- You want to live the life you came to live

FREE STRATEGY SESSION

If you are interested in exploring deeper or are curious about our program, schedule a free discovery session. Just go to the website at comealiveinstitute.com/contact and complete the form or click on the Schedule a Call button. I look forward to meeting you!

About the Author

J odi Hadsell is a transformation coach and founder of the Come Alive Institute, where she specializes in helping people find and live their passions. She calls herself *the passion archaeologist*.

Jodi has spent her entire career in service to helping people improve their lives. For over twenty years she worked in corporate learning and development, training and coaching employees in some of the largest technology companies in the world, including EDS, Apple, AT&T, and SAP.

In addition, Jodi founded a boutique staffing agency in San Francisco, Muses, Inc., where she was the Head Talent Advocate, focusing on the desires and passions of the talent to find their ideal jobs. This was in direct contrast to what all other agencies were doing at the time. Jodi believes that if the people are happy, then the business will be happy (and successful).

She has designed and facilitated dozens of successful training programs throughout her career, from new hire training to leadership development. She has also spoken at MacWorld, Human Capital Institute (HCI), and Association of Talent Development (ATD) conferences about talent and career development.

While working in the corporate world, Jodi completed years of intense study in energy work and received three mind-body certifications. In 2011 she began her mind-body coaching and therapy practice, where she uses her 5 Developmental Archetypes to help her clients through a deep transformation to live the life they came here to live.

In 2018 Jodi finally decided to leave the corporate world to publish her Come Alive book and program so that she can help as many people as possible transform their lives and find their true passion.

Jodi currently lives in Dallas, Texas, but her wanderlust takes her to foreign lands frequently.

Website: comealiveinstitute.com

Email: info@comealiveinstitute.com

Facebook: https://www.facebook.com/groups/comealivebook